THE HINDU CULTURE SERIES

Hinduism

Frequently Asked Questions

Central Chinmaya Mission Trust

First Edition August 2006 to September 2011 – 13,000 copies
Revised Edition January 2013 to June 2017 – 8,000 copies
Reprint – October 2019 – 1,500 copies

Published by:
Chinmaya Prakashan
The Publications Division of
Central Chinmaya Mission Trust
Sandeepany Sadhanalaya
Saki Vihar Road, Powai, Mumbai 400072, India
Tel.: +91-22-2803 4900
Email: ccmtpublications@chinmayamission.com
Website: www.chinmayamission.com

Distribution Centre in USA:
Chinmaya Mission West
Publications Division
560 Bridgetown Pike, Langhorne, PA 19053, USA
Tel.: 1-888-CMW-READ, (215) 396-0390 Fax: (215) 396-9710
Email: publications@chinmayamission.org
Website: www.chinmayapublications.com

Credits
Cover Image of Mother Durga: Courtesy of Truth Consciousness
www.truthconsciousness.org, © 1990 Truth Consciousness
Cover Design: Bhaskar Raman, Odalis Valdivieso

Designed by: Chinmaya Kalpanam, Mumbai

Printed by: Shree Sai Art, Mumbai

ISBN 978-81-7597-556-9

CONTENTS

10. What are the goals of human life according to Hindu ethics?

11. What are the four āśramas or stages of an individual's life?

12. What is meant by 'caste' in Hinduism?

13. What is the spiritual significance of joining one's palms in namaskāra or namaste?

14. What is the spiritual significance of the marks on the forehead – bindi, tilaka and tripuṇḍra?

PART TWO: SCRIPTURES 19

15. Describe the two main categories of Hindu scriptures: śruti and smṛti.

16. What does Veda mean?

17. How many Vedas are there, what do they deal with, and what sections do they consist of?

18. What are the Upa-vedas, how many are there, and what do they deal with?

19. What are the Vedāṅgas?

20. What are the schools of Hindu philosophy?

21. What does Vedānta mean?

22. Does philosophy of Vedānta include different schools of thought? If so, what are they?

23. How do we reconcile the different schools of philosophy and different approaches to the Truth?

24. What are the three main scriptural sources for a Vedāntin?

25. What are the Upaniṣads?

26. How many Upaniṣads are there?

27. What are the great declarations or mahāvākyas, and where are they found in the Vedas?

28. What are sūtras?

29. What are the *Brahmasūtras*?

30. What is *Śrīmad Bhagavad-gītā*?

31. What are the purāṇas and how many are there?

32. What are the two major historical epics in Hinduism?

33. What is *Śrīmad Bhāgavatam*?

34. What is *Yoga Vāsiṣṭha*?

35. What are the dharma-śāstras, how many are there, and who wrote them?

36. Who is Manu and what is a manvantara or the Hindu calculation of time?

51. What is a human being's external and internal composition?

52. Describe in detail the three bodies that make up a human being.

53. What is the antaḥkaraṇa or inner equipment?

54. What is the mind and what are its different aspects?

55. What are the waking, dream and deep sleep states, and what is the state beyond time and space?

56. What is the BMI chart?

57. Who is the jīva, who is Īśvara and what is the relationship between the two?

58. What is māyā?

59. If the jīva is bound by māyā, yet is responsible for the choices that determine his destiny, how much of his life is fate and how much of it is free will?

60. If the jīva is the maker of his own destiny, is there any value in praying to Īśvara?

61. What is Brahman?

62. What additional terms, other than Ātman and Brahman, are used to indicate a human being's true nature?

63. What is spiritual Liberation?

64. What causes an individual to consider himself bound?

80. Is the influence of religion on the masses declining? If not, how can we account for corruption and other such pointers to widespread deterioration in ethical and moral values?

81. The traditional charge against Hinduism is that it is fatalistic and that it inhibits progress by making people slaves to the belief in the inevitability of whatever is to happen. How far is this true? What is the basis of such an accusation, which is being advanced even today by well-meaning and highly educated people?

82. It is said that the greatest strength of Hinduism is its breadth of outlook and that this is also its greatest weakness, in that there are very few common prescribed religious observances obligatory for all, as in other religions. Is it necessary and possible to outline certain basic, minimum observances for all Hindus?

83. Will the fundamental values of Hinduism be in any way affected by the eradication of casteism, toward which a concerted effort is being made now at all levels? If harijanas, who constitute a sizable population among Hindus, are made to feel that their religion exposes them to ridicule, how are they to love that religion? In other words, how can all sections of Hindus be made to take equal interest in, and have the same sense of belonging to, their religion?

84. Hinduism has always renewed or revitalised itself according to the needs of the times. In today's context,

are any corrective measures called for? If so, who will bring them about, and how can they be brought about and made acceptable to the masses?

85. Are fasting and such other dietary regulations necessary for leading a spiritual life? Is a Guru essential for one to enter the spiritual path and attain the goal?

86. Will mantras lose their sanctity if they are not in Sanskrit? There are various saṁskāras prescribed in Hinduism from birth to death. Many of these saṁskāras are not being observed today. Should they not be revived?

87. What is the role of rituals in religion? Are they to be discouraged?

88. What is your view regarding proselytisation? If you were convinced that Hinduism has a great role to play in the world, would you consider adopting proselytisation?

89. Are changes visible in Hinduism's doctrines and in the modes of individual and collective worship as a result of contact with the West?

APPENDIX **91**

Vedas

Upa-vedas

Darśanas: Schools of Philosophy

Śabda-śāstras

Arts and Sciences

Pramāṇas: Means of Knowledge

108 Principal Upaniṣads

Transliteration and Pronunciation Guide

In the book, Devanagari characters are transliterated according to the scheme adopted by the International Congress of Orientalists at Athens in 1912. In it one fixed pronunciation value is given to each letter; f, q, w, x and z are not called to use.

Devanagari	Translit-eration	Sounds Like	Devanagari	Translit-eration	Sounds Like
अ	a	son	ढ्	ḍh	adhesive*
आ	ā	father	ण्	ṇ	under*
इ	i	different	त्	t	tabla
ई	ī	feel	थ्	th	thumb
उ	u	full	द्	d	this
ऊ	ū	boot	ध्	dh	Gandhi
ऋ	ṛ	rhythm*	न्	n	nose
ॠ	ṝ	**	प्	p	pen
ऌ	ḷ	**	फ्	ph	phantom*
ए	e	evade	ब्	b	boil
ऐ	ai	delight	भ्	bh	abhor
ओ	o	core	म्	m	mind
औ	au	now	य्	y	yes
क्	k	calm	र्	r	right
ख्	kh	khan	ल्	l	love
ग्	g	gate	व्	v	very
घ्	gh	ghost	श्	ś	shut
ङ्	ṅ	ankle*	ष	ṣ	sugar
च्	c	chuckle	स्	s	simple
छ्	ch	witch*	ह्	h	happy
ज्	j	justice	ं	ṁ	improvise
झ्	jh	Jhansi	:	ḥ	**
ञ्	ñ	banyan	क्ष्	kṣ	action
ट्	ṭ	tank	त्र्	tr	three*
ठ्	ṭh	**	ज्ञ्	jñ	gnosis
ड्	ḍ	dog	ऽ	’	a silent ‘a’

* These letters don’t have an exact English equivalent. An approximation is given here.
** These sounds cannot be approximated in English words.

PREFACE

Chinmaya Mission is pleased to release *Hinduism: Frequently Asked Questions* as a part of The Hindu Culture Series. This book is based on Chinmaya Mission's earlier publication, *Our Heritage*, by R. S. Nathan (Swami Nityananda).

To help young students of Indian culture gain a better understanding of the glory of Sanātana-dharma, more commonly referred to today as Hinduism, in July 1967, Chinmaya Mission published a trimonthly series of booklets entitled *Our Heritage.* Eventually, select topics and ten booklets, with most of the questions and answers authored by R. S. Nathan and a few compiled from various sources, were published as one volume.

His Holiness Swami Chinmayananda, the founder and head of Chinmaya Mission, impressed with the acclaimed publication, sent out 500 copies to Mission workers, devotees, and patrons in India and abroad. Though the series was mainly intended for Chinmaya Bālavihāra and Chinmaya Yuvākendra (Chinmaya mission's children's and youth wings, respectively), adults also found the information useful.

The information in this new reference text is vast, but by no means comprehensive. Suggested reading for further study has been included in some instances. Complementary works from Chinmaya Publications include *Hindu Culture: An Introduction, The Holy Gītā, Meditation & Life, Self Unfoldment, Tattvabodha, In Indian culture* and *Why Do We.*

We thank Rupali Gupta, Rudite Emir, Swami Advayananda, and the Chinmaya International Foundation for their time and effort in bringing out this new publication.

Chinmaya Mission West
Central Chinmaya Mission Trust
August 2006

PART ONE
FUNDAMENTAL CONCEPTS

PART ONE:
FUNDAMENTAL CONCEPTS

1. What is the aim of the Hindu religion?

The aim of the Hindu religion is Self-realisation (Ātmajñāna), or God-realisation (Brahmajñāna), the knowledge of Oneness. Various terms, all leading to the same goal of Oneness, can be used to state this aim:

- Intuition of the Reality: Brahma-anubhava
- Insight into the Truth: Brahma-darśana
- Contact with the Supreme: Brahma-saṁsparśa
- Direct apprehension of the Reality: Brahma-sākṣātkāra

2. What is the Hindu concept of God?

God is Brahman, the One, the changeless Truth or Reality. As Brahman cannot be conceived by the intellect, it cannot be defined; it can only be indicated (see Question 61).

With respect to creation, God is the changeless substratum supporting the changing universe. Example: The god of waves is the ocean; the god of ornaments is gold; the god of pots is mud; the god of shirts is cotton. God is thus the cause and the effect. The effect is nothing but the cause in another form. And if the cause is removed, the effect ceases to exist.

Hinduism also refers to God as the Trinity – Brahmā (the creator), Viṣṇu (the sustainer), and Śiva (the destroyer). God is supremely intelligent, ultimate cause from which the entire universe has emerged, in which the universe exists, and into which it eventually dissolves.

It is important to note that Hinduism is not polytheistic (belief in many gods, each a separate entity). Based on varying schools of Hindu philosophy, Hinduism can be called as monotheistic (belief in one God, manifesting different powers in different forms, where there is a dualistic relationship between God and the individual) or monist (belief in one God expressing as all forms, where God alone is or Oneness alone is, and all of the creation is but a manifestation of the one Reality).

3. Why is the Hindu religion called Sanātana-dharma and who founded it?

Sanātana means 'eternal.' Dharma is a word that defies exact translation in English or any other language, but can be said to mean 'the values of life that sustain us.' Therefore, Sanātana-dharma is that religion which is based on life's eternal (universal) values.

By its literal meaning alone, it is clear that Sanātana-dharma is not a religion founded by any historical figure. It is based on eternal truths – principles and values of life –

that hold true for all people, in all places, at all times – past, present and future.

4. Explain in detail the meaning of the word dharma.

In the progress of Indian philosophical thought, the word dharma has acquired such a comprehensive and complex significance that it is almost impossible to define or articulate it in any other language. One description of dharma is 'the law of being.' The essential characteristic of a thing, without which it cannot remain as that thing, is its dharma.

Example: The sweetness of sugar, the luminosity of the sun, the heat of fire, the coolness of water, and the divine Spark of Existence in the human being.

Dharma can be viewed at two levels – cosmic and individual. At the cosmic level, the dharma of totality is called Sanātana-dharma, which is eternal and common to all individuals, at all times. At the societal level, Sanātana-dharma translates into a code of fundamental values that govern our daily lives (see Question 35). At the individual level, a person's svadharma (own dharma) is based on his stage and position in life, and on his vāsanās (inherent tendencies).

Dharma is ethics and religion combined. In general, it stands for all those ideals, purposes, influences, institutions, and ways of conduct that shape the character and evolution of a person, both as an individual and as a member of society. Dharma is the law of right living, the observance of which fulfills two objectives: happiness in life and Liberation from all bondage.

Dhāraṇāt iti dharmam, 'That which sustains is dharma' (*Mahābhārata*). *Mahābhārata*, which is a veritable encyclopedia of Indian wisdom, culture and tradition, emphatically states, 'Nobody has ever violated the principles of dharma without ultimately courting disaster.' The text further states that adharma (unethical action) may carry a man to heights of power and prosperity for a time, but these gains are all temporary and eventually lead to his downfall.

5. What are the fundamental doctrines of Hinduism?

- The Vedas are the ultimate scriptural authority: The Vedas are divine sources of knowledge that reveal the eternal Truth.

- The Self is One, and is independent of the body, mind, and intellect: The human being is, in essence, neither the gross physical body, nor the subtle mind and intellect, but something beyond them. He is the Ātman or the Self, the real Being behind the apparent individual.

- The doctrine of karma: The law of karma (the law of causality) states that we are the creators of our own destiny. Our present condition is due to our past conduct, and our future state will be based on our past as well as present thoughts and actions.

- The doctrine of reincarnation: The essential Self is, by nature, divine, pure, perfect, infinite and free. It was never created and therefore will never die. However, the individual being (jīvātman) that one presently thinks oneself to be, due to ignorance, passes from body to body (reincarnates in different forms) in its onward journey to the realisation of its perfection. For further study, see Chapter 2 of *The Holy Gītā* by Swami Chinmayananda.

- The existence of God as the creator, sustainer, and destroyer, with reference to the world of names and forms: God manifests Himself as the creative and preserving power of the whole universe, and unto Him, the universe returns. The entire phenomenal world rises, exists, dissolves, and again rises in Him. The three functions of creation, preservation and dissolution are but different aspects of the same supreme Being. When we think of Him as the creator, we call Him Brahmā; when we think of Him as the preserver, we call Him Viṣṇu; and when we think of Him as the (constructive) destroyer, we call Him Śiva.

6. Why does Hinduism say that the human being is, in essence, divine (Ātman)?

Hindus believe that the human being is essentially divine. Every human being – irrespective of caste, creed, colour, gender, and so on – can attain the knowledge of this Truth and make his life an expression of It. Perfection is not only open to all, but it is the very nature of all. It has only to be unfolded, revealed. There is no such thing as spiritual death.

The Vedas logically and conclusively prove that the essence of every human being is the one Ātman (Self). Logical thought reveals that a human being is not the body, the mind or the intellect. He is something beyond these instruments, functioning through the body, the mind and the intellect.

This is evident in our daily usage of such expressions as 'my body,' 'my mind' and so on. If I am the owner of the body, mind, and so on, I must be other than the body, mind, and so on.

Example: The statement, 'This is my car' clearly shows that I am not the car, because the car is an object of my perception.

When I apply the same thought process to 'my body,' 'my mind, and so on', I must conclude that the body, mind, and so on are my possessions, not my true being. By disidentifying with my instruments and related objects or persons, I will reach my essential source, which cannot be denied or negated. For further study, see *Self Unfoldment* by Swami Chinmayananda.

7. What are the two doctrines of karma and reincarnation, and why do Hindus believe in them?

Hindus believe in the two doctrines of karma and reincarnation because these doctrines not only logically explain unusual occurrences, but also shed light on life's day-to-day events. Hindus do not consider life and death to be mutually exclusive, but as intertwined and inseparable, like two sides of the same coin. If there are disparities between two individuals at birth, and we see that there are, then the cause for these disparities must have preceded birth.

- Karma: The word karma means 'action.' In accordance with the cosmic laws of karma, each individual reaps the fruits of his actions, performed in this life or in former lives. This logically explains the disparities in creation, that is, between various individuals' environments and situations. No deed, small or great, good or bad, can be without an effect – this is the law of karma, the law of causality.

Karma is not fate. Fate implies the helplessness of a human being to determine his own destiny. The law of karma states that the individual is the creator of his own destiny because his conscious choices in life determine his actions and the fruits thereof.

- Reincarnation: Hindus believe that the jīva or the individual being, travels from life to life, acquiring bodies and environments best suited to exhaust his vāsanās or innate tendencies that are expressed as desires, emotions, and actions. The exhaustion of vāsanās allows the jīva to reach his ultimate goal: complete freedom from the cycle of birth and death through the realisation of his true nature as the Self, or Brahman.

8. What determines whether an act is a merit (puṇya) or a sin (pāpa)?

There are different types of karmas, or actions:

- Nitya karmas (daily duties)
- Naimittika karmas (special duties)
- Kāmya karmas (desire born actions)
- Niṣiddha karmas (wrongful actions)
- Prāyaścitta karmas (actions of penance to improve oneself)

Karmas are performed through three instruments:

- Manas (mind)
- Vāk (speech)
- Kāyā (body)

The results of karmas can be seen in these three categories:

- Puṇya karmas (meritorious, or dhārmika actions, leading to good results)
- Pāpa karmas (wrong, or adhārmika actions, leading to bad results)
- Miśra karmas (actions having mixed results)

Karmas by mind (thoughts): Noble thoughts about bhakti (devotion),vairāgya (dispassion), charity, spiritual evolution, and so on, are mental puṇya karmas. Lustful thoughts pertaining to sense enjoyments, harming others and disrespect for the scriptures, traditions, and dharma are mental pāpa karmas. An admixture of both types is known as miśra karma. In simple terms, Swami Chinmayananda explains puṇya karmas as 'self congratulatory acts' and pāpa karmas as 'self insulting acts.'

Karmas by speech (words): Regularly reciting or reading the scriptures, chanting mantras and hymns, singing devotional songs, speaking truthful and noble words, offering others words of love, compassion, and so on, are puṇya karmas performed by speech.

Words of disrespect for the scriptures, verbal abuse of the Lord and Mahātmās, engaging in lies or cruel, offensive and, unsympathetic talk, and so on are pāpa karmas of speech.

Karmas by body (actions): Bathing in holy waters, prostrating to the Guru, the Lord and saintly persons, performing worship (pūjās), seeking the presence of holy beings, submitting to tapas (sacrifice and discipline), and so on, are puṇya karmas of the body.

Immoral acts, causing injury to others, indulging in cruelty, associating with cruel persons, and so on, are pāpa karmas of the body.

Troubling others while doing a good deed, misappropriation of another's wealth or property in the process of doing good work (for example, building temples, giving charity), not giving proper remuneration for services rendered, and so on, are all miśra karmas of the body.

Vedavyāsa has said, "Paropakārāya puṇyāya pāpāya parapīḍanam", "Doing good to others at any of these three levels of body, speech, and mind is puṇya. Injuring others at any of these levels is pāpa." Puṇya is that which helps us evolve and pāpa is that by which we devolve or by which our progress stagnates. For further study, see *The Holy Gītā* by Swami Chinmayananda.

9. What is the Hindu concept of heaven and hell?

The Hindu concept of heaven and hell can be understood at different levels: physical and mental. Beyond these two levels, which are relative, is the absolute standpoint.

- At the physical level: The purāṇas expound on 14 different dimensions in God's creation, where heaven and hell exist as separate planes of existence. The realms of heaven and hell are described in detail in the scriptures and are planes where jīvas (individuals) exist in their subtle bodies.

  Heaven (svarga) is a plane where departed jīvas go to reap the fruits of their virtuous deeds and remain there until their merits are exhausted. In heaven, one knows no hunger, thirst, or disease, for there is no physical body. The enjoyments in heaven are more intense, subtle, and refined, but they still cannot give everlasting peace and bliss. The period for which the jīva stays in heaven depends upon the degree of his past meritorious deeds on earth.

  The purāṇas speak of hell (naraka) as a plane where evildoers suffer for a period, in accordance with the fruits of their actions. It is presided over by Lord Yama, or the Lord of death. The punishment meted out in hell is reformatory and educative, and is not remembered by the jīva upon rebirth.

  Hindus do not believe in a permanent state of heaven and hell; they are both transitory. An individual goes to heaven or hell depending on his past actions and, after exhausting his merits or demerits, comes back to earth to strive for mokṣa, or liberation from the cycle of birth and death. The planes of heaven and hell are thus intermediate stages in the individual's progress toward final Liberation. For further study, see *Śrīmad Bhāgavatam*.

- <u>At the mental level:</u> From a subtler standpoint, heaven and hell are mental realms or fields of experience. When one's mind is filled with contentment, patience, compassion, forgiveness, and similar values, one experiences a great degree of joy and lives in his own 'heaven.' When one's mind is filled with negativities, such as anger, greed, jealousy, and so on, life is miserable and one is living in a self created 'hell.' Thus, both heaven and hell are mental creations.

- <u>From the absolute standpoint:</u> At the absolute level, both heaven and hell are only projections of the mind, just as this waking world of names and forms is but a projection, born out of ignorance, on Brahman. Heaven and hell are given relative reality only as long as the sense of individuality (ego) persists – as long as the individual has not realised his true Self. From the absolute standpoint of Oneness, there is nothing other than the one Reality. For further study, see *Māṇḍūkya-upaniṣad*.

There are four goals of human life called puruṣārthas:

- Dharma: righteous action.
- Artha: acquisition of wealth and worldly possessions.
- Kāma: fulfilment and enjoyment of desires.
- Mokṣa: liberation from the cycle of birth and death.

Dharma is listed as the first puruṣārtha because artha and kāma are to be obtained through methods sanctioned by the tenets of dharma. Mokṣa is the highest of the puruṣārthas and is the ultimate goal of human life (see Question 63).

11. What are the four āśramas, or stages, of an individual's life?

- Brahmacarya: the stage of living as a brahmacārī, a student or an ardent disciple.
- Gṛhastha: the stage of living as a householder.
- Vānaprastha: the stage of living as a hermit.
- Sannyāsa: the stage of living as a renunciate.

Every human being is enjoined to go through all these stages in succession. Based on a 100 year life span, an average person would go through the stages as follows: 0-25 years – brahmacarya; 25-50 years – gṛhastha; 50-75 years – vānaprastha; 75-100 years – sannyāsa. By going through these stages, an individual discharges his familial and societal obligations, and finally liberates himself. It should be noted that there are guided or advanced spiritual seekers who bypass some stages and go directly to sannyāsa because of their intense desire for Liberation.

A person who has entered the stage of sannyāsa is called a sannyāsī. Lord Kṛṣṇa defines sannyāsa in *Bhagavad-gītā* 18.2 as the renunciation of all kāmya karmas, or actions performed with a desire for the fruits thereof. Internal sannyāsa is an inner transformation, the renunciation of all desires. External sannyāsa refers to the renunciation of all external bonds and attachments for those seekers who want to, and are fit to, devote their lives to a spiritual pursuit.

12. What is meant by 'caste' in Hinduism?

The words 'caste' and 'caste system' are attributed to Hinduism, but are greatly misinterpreted and misunderstood concepts in society today. The caste system of today is the result of generations trying to preserve their knowledge, profession, social status, and so on, by misusing and misinterpreting the scriptures for personal convenience. As the word is used today, caste is a categorisation based on birth, profession, or social status. However, the scriptures do not condone this interpretation.

The Hindu scriptures expound on the three guṇas (inner dispositions): sattva (expressed as creativity, inspiration, mental quietude, and so on), rajas (expressed as restlessness, dynamism, mental agitation, and so on), and tamas (expressed as laziness, negligence, dullness, and so on). An individual's personality is comprised of changing permutations and combinations of these three guṇas, which expresses at the mental level as thoughts and at the physical level as actions.

In *Śrīmad Bhagavad-gītā*, Lord Kṛṣṇa states that a person's disposition is of his own making, the result of his own choices and actions. *Bhagavad-gītā* uses the term varṇa or colour to describe an individual's personality and based on the three guṇas, categorises humanity into four varṇas or castes:

- Brāhmaṇas (Brahmins): The thinkers, who have a preponderance of sāttvika qualities on a rājasika base, whose duty is to lead society along the righteous path and be role models in secular and spiritual matters.

- Kṣatriyas: The leaders or warriors, with a preponderance of rājasika qualities on a sāttvika base, whose duty is to protect and nurture society.
- Vaiśyas: The businessmen or financiers, with a preponderance of rājasika qualities on a tāmasika base, whose duty is to fulfil society's economic needs.
- Śūdras: The labourers, with a preponderance of tāmasika qualities on a rājasika base, whose duty it is to contribute labour for society's progress and well-being.

Gītā teaches that one's varṇa is not based on one's birth, lineage, or profession, and therefore, no one can be deemed superior or inferior in society based on these superficial factors. One's varṇa is determined by which guṇas one chooses to develop and express. At any given time, each individual falls primarily into one of the four varṇas, based on his predominant tendencies. However, there is always room for change and growth. The highest goal is to recognise the one Spirit behind all the veils of varṇa. For further study, see *The Holy Gītā* by Swami Chinmayananda.

13. What is the spiritual significance of joining one's palms in namaskāra or namaste?

The traditional Hindu greeting of namaskāra or namaste is for one and all, and is done by reverently joining the palms at the chest and humbly bowing the head. Namaskāra is a form of prostration and salutation, and has profound spiritual significance.

In Sanskrit, namaḥ + te = namaste. It means, 'I bow to you; my prostrations and salutations to you.' Namaḥ can also be literally interpreted as na mama, meaning, 'not mine.' The purpose of saying namaste is thus to negate one's ego (sense of separateness) and to recognise the divine in every person we greet. The life force, Self or Lord in me, is the same in all. The joining of the palms depicts this sense of Oneness. When we know this significance, our greeting paves the way for a deeper, divine communion, complete with love and respect.

14. What is the spiritual significance of the marks on the forehead – bindi, tilaka and tripuṇḍra?

The bindi, tilaka and tripuṇḍra are traditionally applied on the forehead with kumkum (vermilion powder), candan (sandalwood paste) or bhasma (sacred ash).

The bindi or tilaka (dot or vertical line applied between the eyebrows) symbolises the third eye of wisdom or enlightenment, which opens when the spiritual seeker has purified his mind, made it single pointed, and gone beyond relative existence to merge into pure Consciousness.

The tripuṇḍra (three horizontal lines applied across the forehead) symbolises various triads that the seeker has to transcend: the syllables of Om (or A-U-M) which represent the planes of waking, dream and deep sleep; the guṇas of sattva, rajas, and tamas; the instruments – gross body, subtle body, and causal body; the experiencer, experience, and experienced; and so on. The wearing of the bindi, tilaka, or tripuṇḍra thus serves as a constant reminder to the seeker of his ultimate goal of Self-realisation.

PART TWO
SCRIPTURES

PART TWO: SCRIPTURES

15. Describe the two main categories of Hindu scriptures: śruti and smṛti.

The sacred books of the Hindus fall under two broad categories: śruti and smṛti. Hindus believe that the śrutis are God-revealed and eternal, and the smṛtis are man-made, passed down through generations, according to the needs of the time. The śrutis deal with fundamental principles that hold true for all time, while the smṛtis deal with the practical application of those eternal principles according to changing times. In fact, there is a śruti content in every religion.

The word śruti, 'that which is heard,' refers to the Vedas. The word smṛti, 'that which is remembered,' refers to the codes of conduct, set forth in texts like *Manusmṛti*, by which human beings should live.

16. What does Veda mean?

The word Veda comes from the root vid, 'to know.' Veda literally means 'the book of Knowledge.' It is a compendium containing sacred as well as secular knowledge.

17. How many Vedas are there, what do they deal with, and what sections do they consist of?

Veda is one book of Knowledge divided into four portions, but these portions are commonly referred to as the four Vedas, namely:

- *Ṛg-veda*: Hymns of praise; believed to be the oldest book known to humanity and one of the most precious collections of Knowledge.
- *Yajur-veda*: Special directions and formulas for the preparation and performance of rituals and ceremonies.
- *Sāma-veda*: Melodies and songs, with precise intonations and modulations, to be chanted at rituals; the most voluminous of the four Vedas.
- *Atharva-veda*: Mystical formulas; tantrika and other forms of esoteric knowledge, which paved the way for modern science in India.

Each Veda consists of three sections, namely:

- Saṁhitās: The mantra portion, consisting of hymns of praise for Vaidika deities.
- Brāhmaṇas: The ritualistic portion, dealing with the methodology of performing Vaidika rituals.
- Āraṇyakas: The contemplative portion, including the Upaniṣads

18. What are the Upa-vedas, how many are there, and what do they deal with?

The Upa-vedas or Veda upāṅgas are writings subordinate to the Vedas. They are four in number, one attached to each of the four Vedas:

- In *Ṛg-veda*: *Āyurveda*, the science of medicine and health.
- In *Yajur-veda: Dhanurveda*, military science.
- In *Sāma-veda: Gandharvaveda*, the art and science of music.
- In *Atharva-veda: Sthāpatyaveda*, the science of mechanics and construction.

19. What are the Vedāṅgas?

There are six Vedāṅgas that are the additional limbs of the Vedas:

- Chandas: Prosody (science of poetic meters).
- Jyotiṣa: Astronomy and astrology.
- Kalpa: Construction and design of religious sites.
- Nirukta: Vaidika etymology.
- Śikṣā: Phonetics.
- Vyākaraṇa: Grammar.

20. What are the schools of Hindu philosophy?

There are six darśanas, or schools, of Hindu philosophy, each independent of the other, but each accepting the Vedas as the scriptural authority:

- Nyāya of Sage Gautama: Deals with the Hindu system of logic.
- Vaiśeṣika of Sage Kaṇāda: Deals with the atomic theory and structure of the universe.
- Sānkhya of Sage Kapila: Deals with the relationship between Nature and Spirit as the cause of the world.
- Yoga of Sage Patañjali: Deals with gaining mastery over oneself through the transformation of one's inner equipment.
- Mīmāṁsā of Sage Jaimini: Deals with the procedure and practice of rituals – a treatise on karmakāṇḍa; also known as Pūrva Mīmāṁsā.
- Vedānta of Sage Kṛṣṇa Dvaipāyana Bādarāyaṇa Vyāsa (Sage Vedavyāsa): Deals with the philosophical and theological views in the Upaniṣads; also known as Uttara Mīmāṁsā.

21. What does Vedānta mean?

The term Vedānta means:

- Veda + anta, 'the end of the Vedas,' which literally means the concluding portion of the Vedas, but refers to the end goal indicated by the Vedas: Brahman.

- Vede siddhyati siddhānta iti vedānta, 'the philosophical conclusions arrived at, by, and in the Vedas'.

22. Does philosophy of Vedānta include different schools of thought? If so, what are they?

The Hindu seers (ṛṣis) were never satisfied unless they discussed every question to its logical and irrefutable conclusion. This led to different schools of philosophical thought.

There were six schools of thought of Vedānta that developed over time, all claiming to be based on teachings of Upaniṣads. They are (in chronological order, from the earliest):

- Advaita of Ādi Śaṅkarācārya.
- Viśiṣṭādvaita (Viśiṣṭa-advaita) of Rāmānujācārya.
- Dvaita of Madhvācārya.
- Śuddhādvaita (Śuddha-advaita) of Vallabhācārya.
- Dvaitādvaita (Dvaita-advaita) of Nimbārkācārya.
- Acintyabhedābheda (Acintya-bheda-abheda) of Jīva Gosvāmin.

23. How do we reconcile the different schools of philosophy and different approaches to the Truth?

The apparently divergent scriptures have been given by different teachers at different periods of time to suit different types of students. Amidst this diversity, one finds that although the paths are different, the goal is the same. Each teacher vehemently emphasises a path that is best suited for the benefit of his disciples. A true student is able to see through these apparent differences and remain firm on his own path.

Different schools of philosophy are merely different notions about, and interpretations of, the same subject. Differences will exist when teachers and scriptures are trying to describe the indescribable.

Gavāmaneka varṇānāṁ kṣīrasya-api-eka-varṇatā,
kṣīravat paśyate jñānam liṅginastu gavām yathā.
Cows are of different colours,
but the milk from all the cows is the same colour – white.

– *Amṛtabindu-upaniṣad - verse 19*

So too, the intelligent one should regard knowledge as the milk and the sources of such knowledge as the cows.

Scriptures may differ in words and interpretations, but all speak of and indicate the same Truth. The milk is of the main concern for the cowherd; so too, knowledge (not its source), should be the main concern for the sincere seeker.

24. What are the three main scriptural sources for a Vedāntin?

Prasthāna-traya refers to the three sources of scriptural authority for a Vedāntin. These are:

- Upaniṣads
- *Brahmasūtras*
- *Śrīmad Bhagavad-gītā*

These are the three accepted sources from which the different schools of Vedānta derive their authority. Of the prasthāna-traya, the *Brahmasūtras* are nyāya pramāṇa (means of knowledge with an emphasis on logic); the *Bhagavad-gītā* is smṛti pramāṇa (means of knowledge with an emphasis on the smṛtis); and the Upaniṣads are śruti pramāṇa (means of knowledge with an emphasis on the śrutis).

25. What are the Upaniṣads?

The Upaniṣads are the first source of scriptural authority in the prasthāna-traya. The Upaniṣads generally form the end portion of the āraṇyakas of the Vedas, and therefore the philosophy described therein is called Vedānta, which means 'the end of the Vedas.' It is important not to take this definition literally, as Upaniṣads also appear in other sections of the Vedas and are distinguished as such through their subject matter: the supreme Reality. The Upaniṣads are texts that deal with the highest knowledge – the knowledge of the pure Self – and are thus the ultimate teaching, the end goal indicated by the Vedas.

The Upaniṣads contain the essence of Vaidika teachings. They are the foundation on which most of the later philosophies of India rest. There is no important form of spiritual thought originating in India that has not been derived from the Upaniṣads.

The word Upaniṣad consists of three syllables: upa-ni-ṣad, meaning, 'near-below-sit.' This meaning denotes the flow of knowledge from the higher to the lower level, from the Guru to the śiṣya (disciple). The word also reflects the reverential attitude of the śiṣya, who physically sits below the level of the

Guru, near his feet. For further study, see Ādi Śaṅkarācārya's *Vivekacūḍāmaṇi* and introduction to *Kaṭhopaniṣad*.

26. How many Upaniṣads are there?

There are 1,179 Upaniṣads, as follows:

- 21 in *Ṛg-veda*
- 108 in *Yajur-veda*
- 1,000 in *Sāma-veda*
- 50 in *Atharva-veda*

Tradition considers 108 Upaniṣads (see Appendix) as important and authoritative. Of these ten are considered as the major Upaniṣads:

Aitareya	*Kena*
Bṛhadāraṇyaka	*Māṇḍūkya*
Chāndogya	*Muṇḍaka*
Īśāvāsya	*Praṣna*
Kaṭha	*Taittirīya*

27. What are the great declarations or mahāvākyas, and where are they found in the Vedas?

The quintessence of Vedānta is found in 'great declarations' called mahāvākyas. These are numerous and appear throughout the Vedas in different places. There are four popularly known mahāvākyas, culled from four Upaniṣads, one from each of the four Vedas.

Though every mahāvākya is complete by itself and has the potential to grant Liberation to a fit aspirant, a common, sequential storyline to connect the teachings in the four mahāvākyas and provide a roadmap for sādhanā, is given as follows:

- Prajñānam Brahma: 'Consciousness is Brahman.' (*Aitareya-upaniṣad, Ṛg-veda*)

  This first mahāvākya is the lakṣaṇa vākya (statement of definition), for it gives a definition of Truth. It declares that Consciousness, the spiritual core that enlivens each of us, is the same all-pervading Consciousness in all beings and things.

- Tat Tvam Asi: 'That Thou Art.' (*Chāndogya-upaniṣad, Sāma-veda*)

  The disciple, after reflecting on the Guru's teachings, still has doubts. In the second mahāvākya, the upadeśa vākya (statement of instruction), the Guru tells the disciple that he (the disciple) is verily the supreme Brahman and not the limited personality he imagines himself to be.

  Thus, the Truth the disciple is seeking is none other than his own Self and is to be found within. This state of Consciousness is to be realised here and now through Self-inquiry.

- Ahaṁ Brahma Asmi: 'I am Brahman.' (*Bṛhadāraṇyaka-upaniṣad, Yajur-veda*)

  Through meditation, after overcoming his habitual thinking of the Truth as something other than himself, the student comes back to the master filled with his intimate and direct experience of the Truth. His experience is of the nature of this mahāvākya, which is the anubhava vākya (statement of experience).

- Ayaṁ Ātmā Brahma: 'This Self is Brahman.' (*Māṇḍūkya-upaniṣad, Atharva-veda*)

  Once the disciple is established in his real nature, the Guru advises him to constantly revel and abide in the Self. The nature of his abidance is expressed by this mahāvākya, which is the anusandhāna vākya (statement of constant practice).

28. What are sūtras?

Sūtras are systematic treatises in the form of aphorisms. They act as pointers and memory aids for intensive discussions on any topic. *Padma Purāṇa* gives the following requirements for the creation of a sūtra:

- Should be concise to facilitate memorisation.
- Should hold no ambiguity.
- Should give the essence of various viewpoints on a topic, covering all aspects of the question.

- Should use only words that are absolutely necessary, relevant, and meaningful.
- Should be capable of being understood from all perspectives.
- Should not be repetitious.
- Should not have any logical fallacies.

Examples: The *Brahmasūtras* of Vedavyāsa, the *Yogasūtras* of Patañjali, and the *Bhaktisūtras* of Sage Nārada.

29. What are the *Brahmasūtras*?

The *Brahmasūtras*, also known as *Śārīrika sūtras*, are the second source of scriptural authority in the prasthāna-traya. The *Brahmasūtras* are a compendium of 555 aphorisms by Sage Vedavyāsa. The sūtras present, in a concentrated form, the entire philosophy of the Upaniṣads. In this textbook for postgraduate studies of Vedānta, Sage Vyāsa leads the student into the inquiry of the nature of the supreme Reality, the relationship between the human being and the supreme Reality, the ultimate fulfilment of human birth and existence, and the means to realise this fulfilment.

30. What is *Śrīmad Bhagavad-gītā*?

Śrīmad Bhagavad-gītā is the third source of scriptural authority in the prasthāna-traya. *Bhagavad-gītā*, or the 'Lord's Song,' written by Sage Vedavyāsa, is traditionally comprised of 700 ślokas, or verses (1 spoken by Dhṛtarāṣṭra, 41 spoken by Sañjaya, 84 spoken by Arjuna, and 574 spoken by Lord Kṛṣṇa).

There is also a widely accepted version of the *Bhagavad-gītā* that contains 701 verses. The spiritual teacher, Śrī Madhusūdana Sarasvatī, who also authored *Gītā Dhyānam* and the concluding colophon at the end of each *Bhagavad-gītā* chapter, added a question to open Chapter 13. The 18 chapters of the *Bhagavad-gītā* are found in *Mahābhārata: Bhīśma Parva* 25 to 42.

Śrīmad Bhagavad-gītā is the most popular, profound, and poetic philosophical composition in Sanskrit literature. It is said to be perhaps the only philosophical song of its kind existing in any known language. It is a text that conveys sublime spiritual teachings and the art of living. If the hold that a specific work has on the mind of a human being is any indication of its importance, then *Śrīmad Bhagavad-gītā* is the most influential work in Indian thought. It is the only philosophical treatise in the world that was delivered on a battlefield and, as such, also has great allegorical significance. Its teaching is timeless; it is applicable at a universal level and addresses humanity everywhere, at all times, in all aspects.

31. What are the purāṇas and how many are there?

There are 18 purāṇas and they generally deal with these five topics:

- Sarga: Primary creation or cosmogony.
- Pratisarga: Secondary creation, sustenance, destruction, and re-creation of worlds, including chronology.
- Vaṁśa: Genealogy of deities and patriarchs.

- Manvantara: Reigns of the different Manus.
- Vaṁśānucarita: History of the solar and lunar dynasties, and their descendants.

The 18 mahāpurāṇas are divided into three categories of s ix each:

- *Brāhmapurāṇas: Brahma, Brahmāṇḍa, Brahma-vaivarta, Bhaviṣya, Mārkaṇḍeya, Vāmana;*
- *Vaiṣṇavapurāṇas: Viśṇu, Bhāgavata, Garuḍa, Nāradīya, Padma, Varāha;*
- *Śaivapurāṇas: Śiva (Vāyu), Agni, Kūrma, Liṅga, Matsya, Skanda;*

In addition to these 18 purāṇas, there are 46 upa-purāṇas. Of the 46 upa-purāṇas, 18 are prominent:

Bhārgava	*Kālikā*	*Sanatkumāra*
Brihannāradīya	*Kapila*	*Śiva-rahasya*
Devī Bhāgavata	*Nandi*	*Sūrya*
Durvāsa	*Narasiṁha*	*Vāmana*
Gaṇeśa	*Parāśara*	*Varuṇa*
Haṁsa	*Sāmba*	*Vāsiṣṭha*

32. What are the two major historical epics in Hinduism?

Rāmāyaṇa and *Mahābhārata* are the two itihāsas or historical sagas, that serve as an inspiration for humanity and exemplify the realisation of the four puruṣārthas: dharma (righteous and dutiful living), artha (wealth), kāma (desire fulfilment), and mokṣa (Liberation).

- *Rāmāyaṇa* literally means 'the abode of Rāma' and it is the smaller of the two works. The epic mirrors the highest ideals of Hindu tradition, culture and civilisation. The story, which took place in Tretāyuga (one of the four ages of the world; see Question 36), centers on Rāma, the prince of Ayodhyā and the incarnation of Lord Viṣṇu, and his wife Sītā, the incarnation of mother Lakśmī. *Rāmāyaṇa* sings the Lord's glories and instructs humanity on how to lead a fulfilling life and attain the four puruṣārthas. The epic is profound and timeless in its popularity, and teaches, with the use of symbolism, how an individual can evolve to greatness and perfection.

  Sage Vālmīki's *Rāmāyaṇa* has been translated into most Indian languages, as well as several foreign languages, including Russian It consists of 24,000 stanzas in seven cantos, and depicts Rāma as the ideal king, son, brother, friend, and husband. In Bharata, Lakṣmaṇa, and Śatrughna, we see exemplified the ideal brothers. In Sītā, we have the purest flower of Indian womanhood who is devoted to her Lord in thought, word, and deed.

  Rāmāyaṇa is an ideal textbook of morals and values that inspires nobler dimensions of character and conduct. Other noteworthy and famous versions of *Rāmāyaṇa* include Sage Vedavyāsa's *Adhyātma Rāmāyaṇa*, Gosvāmī Tulasīdāsa's *Śrī Rāmacaritamānasa* (*Tulasī Rāmāyaṇa*), and Kambar's *Kamba Rāmāyaṇa*.

- *Mahābhārata* is an epic that is more than eight times the size of Homer's *Iliad* and *Odyssey* combined, and in philosophical content is unparalleled to any other literary work in the world. This grand book of knowledge contains more than 100,000 stanzas in 18 chapters and is the work of the renowned Sage Vedavyāsa.

The underlying theme of *Mahābhārata* is 'yato dharmaḥ tato jayaḥ,' 'where there is dharma, there is victory,' indicating the ultimate triumph of good over evil and the establishment of righteousness. The story unfolds towards the end of Dvāparayuga and describes the genealogy and events leading upto, and after, the familial war between royal cousins.

The story is used as a vehicle to convey eternal philosophical truths of the highest order. It is said, "That which is in *Mahābhārata* can be seen elsewhere, but that which is not therein cannot be seen anywhere else." This gives an idea of the comprehensiveness of subjects in the epic, which is full of lofty instructions on all aspects of human life and endeavour – an inspiring saga of India's past glory, portraying all that is great and noble in humanity.

The guiding spirit throughout the epic is the divine figure of Lord Kṛṣṇa, who brings the pure and the righteous to Himself, and who destroys evil and evildoers. *Śrīmad Bhagavad-gītā* or the 'Lord's Song,' is part of *Mahābhārata*.

33. What is *Śrīmad Bhāgavatam*?

The Sanskrit term Bhāgavata means 'pertaining to the Lord': He who has (the six) glories. *Śrīmad Bhāgavata Purāṇa*, or *Śrīmad Bhāgavatam*, is commonly referred to as *Bhāgavata*, or *Bhāgavatam*, and it is undoubtedly the most voluminous and popular of the purāṇas.

This devotional text portrays the sagas of Lord Viṣṇu's various avatāras (incarnations), focusing on the life of Lord Kṛṣṇa. *Śrīmad Bhāgavatam* remains unrivalled in its stories, expressions, and teachings on devotion, knowledge, and action, all dedicated to the Divine.

34. What is *Yoga Vāsiṣṭha*?

Yoga Vāsiṣṭha is a book of 36,000 verses from the pen of the celebrated Sage Vālmīki, the author of *Rāmāyaṇa*. Sage Vasiṣṭha's spiritual teachings and advice to Śrī Rāma comprise the subject matter of this highly philosophical treatise. The method employed by Sage Vasiṣṭha is unique, as he conveys profound philosophical truths to Śrī Rāma through the narration of innumerable stories.

35. What are the dharma-śāstras, how many are there, and who wrote them?

The dharma-śāstras are works by various sages. They are social laws that include the codes of conduct to be observed by individuals throughout their lives.

Manu's dharma-śāstra, also known as *Manusmṛti,* is the fundamental dharma-śāstra that is applicable to the entire manvantara (time period until the appearance of the next Manu; see Question 36). *Manusmṛti* forms the basis of Hindu law.

Additionally, there are 18 specific dharma-śāstras that are applicable in different periods of time. The 18 dharma-śāstras are named after their authors:

Āpastamba	*Likhita*	*Śaunaka*
Bharadvāja	*Parāśara*	*Vāsiṣṭha*
Dakṣa	*Samakha*	*Viṣṇu*
Devala	*Saṁvarta*	*Vyāsa*
Gautama	*Śatānīka*	*Yājñavalkya*
Harita	*Śaṭotraya*	*Yama*

36. Who is Manu and what is a manvantara, or the Hindu calculation of time?

Antara means 'space' or 'duration between.' Therefore, a manvantara is the period of time or duration that a Manu (the archetypal human being) rules the entire creation. Hindus calculated time based on manvantaras. Western scientists and archaeologists later discovered that these manvantaras are based on accurate astronomical calculations.

One manvantara is calculated as follows:

- 360 human years make one divya varṣa (celestial year).
- 4,800 divya varṣas make one 'Satyayuga', or 'Kṛtayuga'.
- 3,600 divya varṣas make one 'Tretāyuga'.
- 2,400 divya varṣas make one 'Dvāparayuga'.
- 1,200 divya varṣas make one 'Kaliyuga'.

All the yugas together total 12,000 divya varṣas, and this one cycle of all the yugas makes one mahāyuga or caturyuga. One manvantara = 71 mahāyugas or 306,720,000 human years. One kalpa or cycle of creation, preservation and destruction = 14 manvantaras. Thus, the cycle of time continues.

At the beginning of each manvantara, a Manu appears and codifies all ethical and social regulations to be followed during the manvantara. The Manu whose code is currently being followed is Vaivasvata Manu, who is the seventh in the line of the cycle of 14 Manus. The six Manus who preceded Vaivasvata Manu were: Svāyambhuva, Svārociśa, Uttama, Tāmasa, Raivata, and Cākṣuṣa. The seven who will follow Vaivasvata Manu are: Sāvarṇi, Dakṣa-sāvarṇi, Brahma-sāvarṇi, Dharma-sāvarṇi, Rudra-sāvarṇi, Deva-sāvarṇi, and Indra-sāvarṇi.

37. Is there any special significance of the number 18 in the Hindu scriptures?

Yes. Aside from the fact that there are 18 purāṇas, 18 major upa-purāṇas, and 18 dharma-śāstras, the significance of the number 18 is best illustrated in *Mahābhārata*, which is divided into 18 parvas, or sections. The Mahābhārata war was fought with 18 army divisions: 11 on the Kaurava side and 7 on the Pāṇḍava side. The war lasted 18 days. The treatise *Śrīmad Bhagavad-gītā* is a part of *Mahābhārata* and has 18 chapters. In *Bhagavad-gītā*, Lord Kṛṣṇa describes the ideal man in 18 verses at the end of Chapter 2, in which He lists the 18 traits that are found in a man of steady wisdom.

The theme of all scriptures of all religions in the world is the same: the victory of the higher Self over the lower self, of righteousness over unrighteousness, of good over evil, of dharma over adharma. Vedavyāsa originally titled *Mahābhārata* as *Jaya* (victory). The word jaya is in the opening stanzas of both, *Mahābhārata* and *Bhagavad-gītā*.

In Sanskrit numerology, the Kaṭapayādi system, each letter has a formula-based, numerical value. The numerical value of the word jaya is 18. To stress the importance of the word jaya, the number 18 is given a prominent place not only in *Mahābhārata*, but also throughout various Hindu scriptures. The number 18 is thus repeatedly used as an auspicious reminder : to be alert in our constant battle for inner, spiritual victory.

PART THREE
MANTRAS AND WORSHIP

PART THREE:
MANTRAS AND WORSHIP

38. What does Om mean?

Om is the all-encompassing, sacred symbol that represents the infinite, indefinable Brahman, the Reality indicated by the Vedas, the all-pervading substratum of this universe. Om is praṇava, or God as the primal sound. It is solemnly chanted at the commencement of all prayers and rituals, and is an aid to concentration and contemplation.

Om comprises of three syllables, a-u-m, which represent our three states of experience, namely, waking, dream, and deep sleep. Collectively, Om represents the fourth state, the superconscious state known as 'Turīya'. Om is a vast and subtle subject; for further study, see *Māṇḍūkya-upaniṣad*.

39. What is a mantra?

A mantra is a sacred word or words recited and contemplated upon during worship. Mananāt trāyate iti mantraḥ: 'That (word or phrase) which leads us to the highest Goal through reflection upon it is called a mantra.'

40. What is the Gāyatrī mantra?

Om bhūr bhuvaḥ suvaḥ, Tat savitur vareṇyam,
Bhargo devasya dhīmahi, Dhiyo yo naḥ prachodayāt.

'We meditate on Om, the supreme Reality that pervades the earth, interspace, and the heavens, that is the worshipful and adored Lord Sun, who shines as the light of Consciousness in our intellects. Burn away our ignorance and illumine our intellects [with the wisdom of the highest Truth].'

The Gāyatrī mantra (*Ṛg-veda* 3.62.10) is one of the most ancient and divine hymns, and is the quintessence of the Vedas and Hindu culture. The mantra, originally revealed in meditation to Ṛṣi Viśvāmitra, is a treasure of knowledge in both spiritual and secular fields, for it grants the aspirant cosmic energy, acute intelligence, subtle discrimination, creative vision, healing powers, and, ultimately Self-realisation.

The word gāyatrī literally means gāyantam trāyate iti gāyatrī: 'that [mantra] which protects the one who sings or chants it.' Trāyate also means 'that which takes one across the ocean of transmigration or saves one from the cycle of birth and death.' Chanting the Gāyatrī mantra invokes divinity in a person and blesses him with spiritual illumination. This universal prayer for ultimate enlightenment is not chanted for material gain.

In some ancient texts, the Gāyatrī mantra is also referred to as Sāvitrī-Gāyatrī, indicating that it is an invocation to the Lord in the form of the sun: Lord Sun. Lord Sun represents the giver of Light (Knowledge), the illuminator of all experiences, Ātman. As pure Consciousness, Lord Sun is the core of our being, around whom all our matter envelopments revolve, just as the entire solar system revolves around the sun with mathematical precision. Just as there would be no life on earth without the sun, so too, we would be mere inert matter without the Ātman.

The Gāyatrī mantra is central to the teachings of yoga, Vedānta, āyurveda, and Vaidika astrology. In yoga, it transforms the yogī by stimulating his kuṇḍalinī śakti. To the Vedāntin, it grants Self-knowledge. To the practitioner of āyurveda, the mantra bestows the power of the cosmic prāṇa, which is born of the sun. For the jyotiṣa or astrologer, it grants the knowledge of the movements of the heavenly bodies ruled by the cosmic sun.

The Vaidika metre in which this powerful mantra is composed has also come to be called Gāyatrī. The Gāyatrī metre consists of three lines of eight syllables each.

41. Do Hindus worship idols or images?

Hindus do not worship idols or images per se, but rather the ideals that the idols or images represent. Human beings, with their finite instruments of knowledge, cannot conceive of the formless Infinite, so they use images as aids to concentration. Mahātmā Gandhi said, "An idol does not excite any feeling of veneration in me. But I think that idol worship is part of human nature. We hanker after symbolism. Why should one be more composed in a church than elsewhere? Images are an aid to worship. No Hindu considers an image to be God".

<u>Examples of symbolism in Hinduism:</u> Lord Gaṇeśa's elephant ears represent his ability – selective hearing – to listen to all that is auspicious and worthwhile, and to ignore the rest. Lord Śiva's snakes represent his victory over fear,

death, and ego. Lord Kṛṣṇa's blue color symbolises infinity, like the infinitude of the blue sky. For further study, see *Symbolism in Hinduism* by Swami Chinmayananda.

The names and forms of God may be many, but God is One.

Example: There are many types of golden ornaments, but the essence of all the ornaments is gold. So too, there are many names and forms in the universe, but the essence of all names and forms is One (God).

Devotion, Swami Chinmayananda says, is not 'falling in love,' it is 'rising in love.' Most people need to associate a specific name and form with God because this makes it easier for them to develop a relationship with God. Which name and form each person chooses as his iṣṭa deva, or Lord of his heart, is based on his personal attraction towards that name and form.

42. Can one worship God without the use of images?

Yes, one could worship God as nirguṇa and nirākāra (without qualities and without form). But it is easier to concentrate on God as saguṇa (with form) through a symbol. The Upaniṣads say that the formless Brahman has been assigned forms only for the convenience of the aspirant, as it is not possible for most people to concentrate on that which is formless.

43. Do Hindus worship cows and the natural elements?

Hindus revere cows because they regard all of creation as sacred – whether conscious or inert, whether an animal or a plant. It is not that Hindus worship cows as deities.

Hindus honour cows in gratitude for their generosity, value, and gentleness. The cow is looked upon as a mother, who contributes unconditionally, in so many ways, to the daily sustenance of the human being.

Vaidika hymns do address the natural elements, but the seeker is told to focus on the elements' underlying powers and not merely their physical aspects. Each element has ādhibhautika (physical), ādhidaivika (celestial) and ādhyātmika (spiritual) significance.

Example: Agni signifies fire on the physical plane, purity on the celestial plane, and Light, or God, on the spiritual plane.

44. Who make up the Hindu Trinity?

The Hindu Trinity consists of Brahmā, the creator (note the distinctions between Brahmā, Brahman and brāhmaṇa); Viṣṇu, the sustainer; and Śiva, the destroyer. The three represent the different aspects of the one Brahman, supreme Reality, or God.

It should be noted that the formless One has been assigned such forms only for the convenience of the seeker (sādhakānām hitārthāya brahmaṇo rūpa-kalpanā), whose finite equipment does not allow him to comprehend the infinite, formless One in its entirety.

45. What is meant by avatāra or incarnation of God?

The Sanskrit term avataraṇa means 'coming down' and denotes the manifestation of the Supreme in any form. Lord Kṛṣṇa says in *Śrīmad Bhagavad-gītā* (4.7-4.8):

yadā yadā hi dharmasya glānirbhavati bhārata,
abhyutthānam adharmasya tadātmānam sṛjāmyaham.
paritrāṇāya sādhūnām vināśāya ca duṣkṛtām,
dharma saṁsthāpanārthāya sambhavāmi yuge yuge.

'Whenever righteousness declines and unrighteousness increases, I manifest Myself. I am born from age to age for the protection of the good, for the destruction of evil and evildoers, and for the re-establishment of dharma in the world.'

Thus, the avatāra, which is the incarnation of God in a form – to redeem humanity from spiritual degradation and restore dharma in society – postulates the ultimate victory and supremacy of the Divine.

46. Are all avatāras alike or is there a difference between one avatāra and another?

Not all avatāras are alike. The Lord is ever complete, but His avatāras differ in manifestation, depending on the purpose of the incarnation, the requirements of the time, and the intensity of the circumstances. Based on this, avatāras are categorised as follows:

- Nitya avatāra: The Lord is ever present in the world in the form of saints and sages. Santa Rāmdāsa said, "Those who work for the establishment of dharma are none other than Īśvara Himself."
- Aṁśa avatāra: The Lord manifests with only a part of His potency in order to accomplish a particular goal.

Example: Matsya (fish) avatāra, Varāha (boar) avatāra, Vāmana (dwarf) avatāra, and so on.

- Āveśa avatāra: The Lord suddenly manifests in a situation where a devotee is in need.

  Example: Narasiṁha avatāra, for His devotee Prahlāda.

- Pūrṇa avatāra: The Lord manifests in His full potency and splendour (with all His 16 kalās or attributes). Śrī Kṛṣṇa is a pūrṇa avatāra.

47. What are the avatāras of Lord Viṣṇu?

There have been various avatāras of Lord Viṣṇu; however, it is not possible to give an exact number. This is largely due to the fact that whenever we see a great personality of superhuman strength (physical, mental, intellectual, or spiritual) establishing dharma and achieving great feats, we attribute it to divinity. *Śrīmad Bhāgavatam* states that even though there are countless avatāras, there are 24 avatāras that are significant. The ten renowned manifestations of Lord Viṣṇu are:

Matsya (fish)	Paraśurāma
Kūrma (tortoise)	Rāma
Varāha (boar)	Kṛṣṇa
Narasiṁha (man-lion)	Buddha (or Balarāma)
Vāmana (dwarf)	Kalki

For further study, see *Śrīmad Bhāgavatam.*

PART FOUR
THE MEANS AND THE GOAL

PART FOUR:
THE MEANS AND THE GOAL

48. What are the three dispositions (guṇas) of nature?

- Sattva (sattvaguṇa): good, pious, noble, tranquil.
- Rajas (rajoguṇa): passionate, agitated, authoritative, assertive.
- Tamas (tamoguṇa): dull, inactive, sleepy, ignorant.

These dispositions of nature are seen at the macrocosmic and microcosmic levels of existence. At the microcosmic level, the sum total of all three qualities is always a constant; when one guṇa rises, the others decline. A person's personality or mood at any given time is determined by the preponderance of any one guṇa.

49. What are the five subtle elements or tanmātrās?

The five subtle elements before grossification are known as the tanmātrās: space, air, fire, water and earth. Each tanmātrā is comprised of the three guṇas: sattva, rajas and tamas. Each tanmātrā has a total aspect and an individual aspect.

- The total sāttvika aspects of the five tanmātrās combine to form the antaḥkaraṇa, or inner instrument: manas, buddhi, citta, and ahaṅkāra (see Question 53).

  The individual sāttvika aspects of the five tanmātrās produce the jñāna-indriyas, or sense organs of perception: ears (from space), skin (from air), eyes (from fire), tongue (from water), and nose (from earth).

- The total rājasika aspects of the five tanmātrās combine to form the five prāṇas: prāṇa, apāna, vyāna, udāna, and samāna (see Question 52).

  The individual rājasika aspects of the five tanmātrās produce the karma-indriyas or organs of action: tongue (from space), hands (from air), legs (from fire), genitals (from water), and anus (from earth).

- The individual tāmasika aspects of the five tanmātrās undergo pañcīkaraṇa to form the five elements that make up the gross world.

- The total tāmasika aspects of the five tanmātrās after pañcīkaraṇa combine to form the gross (physical) body.

50. What is pañcīkaraṇa or the grossification process of the five elements?

According to advaita Vedānta, Brahman alone is real and all else is unreal. The concept of creation is described as follows: From the one source, Brahman, come forth the five elements and their combinations to create the phenomenal world. The process by which the five subtle elements (pañca tanmātrās) become the five gross elements (pañca-mahābhūtas), which make up the gross world, is called the five-step division/combination process, or pañcīkaraṇa.

For further study, see *Tattvabodha* by Ādi Śaṅkara, with commentary by Swami Tejomayananda.

51. What is a human being's external and internal composition?

As scientists analyse the objective world without, so too, the philosophers and seekers of Truth study the subjective world within. The ṛṣis (seers) discovered that the human being is composed of:

<u>Three bodies:</u>

- Sthūla śarīra: Gross physical body.
- Sūkṣma śarīra: Subtle body (mind and intellect).
- Kāraṇa śarīra: Causal body.

<u>Four composite personalities:</u>

- Physical
- Mental
- Intellectual
- Spiritual

Five sheaths or layers (corresponding with the three bodies):

- Annamaya kośa or food sheath: The physical body that is born of food, is sustained by food, and returns to the elements to become food again.
- Prāṇamaya kośa, or vital-air sheath: Made up of the five prāṇas, or physiological activities (see Question 52).
- Manomaya kośa, or mental sheath: The mind, which is the seat of emotions.
- Vijñānamaya kośa, or intellectual sheath: The intellect, which is the seat of discrimination and judgment.
- Ānandamaya kośa, or bliss sheath: The state of dreamless deep sleep, which is the seat of blissful ignorance.

52. Describe in detail the three bodies that make up a human being.

The gross body, or sthula śarīra, is:

- Composed of the five elements, or pañca-mahābhūtas (space, air, fire, water and earth), which have undergone the pañcīkaraṇa process (see Question 50).
- Determined by the results of past actions.
- The tenement in which to experience joy (sukha), sorrow (duḥkha), and so on.
- Subject to the six modifications: existence (as a foetus), birth, growth, change, decay, and death

- The basis of relationships like son, father, mother, daughter, and so on.

<u>The subtle body, or sūkṣma śarīra, is:</u>

- Composed of the five elements or pañca-mahābhūtas (space, air, fire, water and earth), which have not undergone the pañcīkaraṇa process.
- Born as and determined by the results of past actions.
- The instrument for experiencing pleasure, pain, and so on.
- Comprised of 17 aspects:
    - 5 jñāna-indriyas, or sense organs of perception: Ears, skin, eyes, tongue, and nose (the respective functional aspects or powers of hearing, touching, seeing, tasting, and smelling).
    - 5 karma-indriyas, or organs of action: Tongue, hands, legs, genitals, and anus (the respective functional aspects or powers of speech, grasping, locomotion, reproduction, and excretion).
    - 5 prāṇas: Prāṇa (inhalation), apāna (exhalation), vyāna (circulation), udāna (the capacity to entertain new thoughts and leave the body at the time of death), and samāna (assimilation); it should be noted that prāṇa and apāna are not restricted to respiratory activities alone.
    - 2 inner instruments: The mind and intellect (two functions of the same equipment; see Question 53).

The causal body, or kāraṇa śarīra, is:

- Inexplicable, beginningless, and in the form of avidyā (ignorance of Reality).
- The abode of all vāsanās (tendencies that compel the jīva to take another birth) and thus the cause for the gross and subtle bodies.
- Unqualified in form and free from thought modifications.

53. What is the antaḥkaraṇa or inner equipment?

The antaḥkaraṇa is the inner equipment of cognition. Its 'mind-stuff' or 'thought stuff' has four facets:

- Manas: Mind (expresses as indecisiveness and agitation).
- Buddhi: Intellect (expresses as decisiveness and rational thinking).
- Citta: Memory.
- Ahaṅkāra: I-thought (sense of individuality, or ego).

54. What is the mind and what are its different aspects?

Mind is the flow of thoughts, or vṛttis. The basis of all thoughts is the I-thought, or aham vṛtti. All thoughts other than the I-thought are known as idam vṛtti. The mind stays in five states:

- Kṣipta: Restless and distracted, wandering from one object to another.

- Mūḍha: Deluded, absorbed in pleasure, or blinded by passion.
- Vikṣipta: Restless and distracted by one object.
- Ekāgra: Single pointed.
- Niruddha: Controlled, with cessation of all thoughts, as in deep sleep.

55. What are the waking, dream, and deep sleep states, and what is the state beyond time and space?

Our three states of experience are known as the avasthā-traya:

- The waking state (jāgrat).
- The dream state (svapna).
- The deep sleep state (suṣupti).

Transcending these three, is the state of God-consciousness called Turīya, one's real nature of inherent divinity. This fourth state is the permanent state of bliss, whereas the former three are temporary states of modification.

Jāgrat-avasthā or waking state: When the jīva, or individual self, through its 14 instruments (five organs of perception, five organs of action, and four facets of the antaḥkaraṇa) perceives the gross objects in their respective fields and interacts with them, the jīva is in the waking state.

Svapna-avasthā, or dream state: The world of experience projected by the mind, as a result of impressions gathered consciously or unconsciously in the waking state, is svapna, or the dream state.

Suṣupti-avasthā, or deep sleep state: This is the state of blissful ignorance. When all instruments cease activity and there is total absence of differentiated knowledge, when even the mind does not function, when Consciousness remains without the duality of subject and object, then the jīva is said to be in the suṣupti, or deep sleep state.

Example using the BMI Chart (see Question 56): The BMI and PFT are totally withdrawn from all OET, but since avidyā (ignorance, in the form of vāsanās) has not been lifted, there is no awareness of pure Consciousness (Om).

Turīya: Turīya is the state of pure Consciousness, where the body, mind, intellect, sense of individuality, objects, emotions, and thoughts do not exist; where avidyā is transcended, and where one's true nature as Brahman reveals.

56. What is the BMI chart?

ॐ

V

↓

B	M	I
↓	↓	↓
P	F	T
↓	↓	↓
O	E	T

Swami Chinmayananda developed the BMI chart to simplify the concepts of advaita Vedānta and describe the relationship between the absolute Reality, the individual self, and the relative world.

The absolute Reality (ॐ or Om) expresses as the individual self (jīva or PFT) because of the force of accumulated vāsanās (V). The Self (Om), through the instruments of body, mind, and intellect (BMI), as if takes on the roles of perceiver, feeler, and thinker (PFT), and interacts with the world of objects, emotions, and thoughts (OET). When the individual transcends all vāsanās, he realises his true Self. For further study, see *Self Unfoldment* by Swami Chinmayananda.

57. Who is the jīva, who is Īśvara, and what is the relationship between the two?

Jīva is defined as: avidyā-upādhiḥ san ātmā jīva iti ucyate, 'The Ātman, as if conditioned by the limitation known as ignorance, is called jīva.' It is this individual jīva that goes in search of happiness with its vāsanās from life to life, body to body.

Īśvara is defined as: māyā-upādhiḥ san Īśvara iti ucyate, 'Awareness, as if conditioned by māyā, is called Īśvara.' Īśvara is another term for God, used with reference to the creation, maintenance and destruction of the universe.

- Jīva: Limited in knowledge, power, and pervasiveness; bound and controlled by māyā.

- Īśvara: Infinite and unlimited in knowledge, power, and pervasiveness; wielder and controller of māyā.

It is important to note that both, jīva and Īśvara are, in essence, Brahman alone. They are described differently only with respect to their associated conditionings.

58. What is māyā?

Sarva-upaniṣad describes māyā as that power which is beginningless and contains within it the seeds to create the entire universe. It is neither real (because it has no power or independent existence separate from Brahman), nor unreal (because it is apparently perceived and experienced in this world through its expressions of āvaraṇa [veiling, non-apprehension] and vikṣepa [agitation, misapprehension]. For further study, see *Tattvabodha.*

59. If the jīva is bound by māyā, yet is responsible for the choices that determine his destiny, how much of his life is fate and how much of it is free will?

Both fate (destiny) and free will are equally at play in our lives at any given time, in past, present, or future. The cycle can be described as follows: Our past actions (free will) determine what we face in the present; this is our self-made destiny. How we face our situations in the present is our free will and this again determines the fate of our future. Basically, we create a blueprint for our future based on our actions in the present.

It is important to note that we ourselves qualify and limit our free will by the vāsanās we cultivate through our actions and habits. There is no point in trying to determine the ratio of free will and destiny at play in any situation. What is needed is to break the cycle by exhausting or transcending all current vāsanās without creating any new ones.

60. If the jīva is the maker of his own destiny, is there any value in praying to Īśvara?

Yes. Prayers full of intense devotion and faith do work, for they invoke the divine power present in each of us. Prayers are not answered based on God's whims and fancies or biases and prejudices. Devotees invoke Īśvara's grace or power through their sincerity, self-effort, faith, and devotion.

61. What is Brahman?

Brahman is the One changeless Truth or Reality. Brahman literally means 'That which is bigger than the biggest' (and is subtler than the subtlest). Brahman cannot be defined, described, or conceived by the intellect. However, to convey at least some idea at the intellectual level, the Upaniṣads give pointers such as:

- Satyam (Truth): That which does not change in the three periods of time (past, present, and future). Despite the appearance of the world of names, and forms, conditioned by time, space, and causation, Brahman remains changeless. Changeless Existence is Sat or Satyam.

- Jñānam (Knowledge): Self-effulgent Consciousness or Awareness (Cit); the principle of knowing without a knower or the known.
- Anantam (Infinite): That which does not have a beginning or an end.
- Ānanda (Bliss): Conscious happiness. The state of unconditioned, objectless (independent) joy, where happiness is not dependent on anything or anyone in the world.

The word Brahman is the Tat aspect when meditating on the mahāvākya 'Tat tvam asi', or 'That thou art' (see Question 27).

62. What additional terms, other than Ātman and Brahman, are used to indicate a human being's true nature?

- Sākṣī: Sākṣī or Witness refers to the pure Awareness that witnesses the world but does not get affected or involved.

  Example: The sun illumines the universe but remains unaffected by it and is not concerned whether it is illumining a palace, a hospital, a prison, or a temple.

  Sākṣī is beyond time, space, and the triad of experiencer, experiencing, and the experienced. It witnesses all thoughts, words, and deeds without interfering with them or being affected by them. This is because there is nothing in the universe other than It.

- Kūṭastha: Kūṭa literally means 'anvil.' All objects that come in contact with the anvil change their form, but the anvil itself remains unchanged; so too, Ātman remains the changeless substratum upon which changes play. The realisation that pure Consciousness alone is, is the state of Kūṭastha.

- Pratyagātman: When the Self shines free from all limiting adjuncts as a brilliant, homogeneous mass of Consciousness, as Existence-Knowledge-Bliss (Sat-Cit-Ānanda), it is called Pratyagātman. Pratyagātman literally means 'inner Self' and indicates the jīva's true nature as Consciousness.

The word Pratyagātman is the tvam aspect when meditating on the mahāvākya 'Tat tvam asi,' or 'That thou art' (see Question 27).

63. What is spiritual Liberation?

Mokṣa, or Liberation, is freedom from all bondage through knowledge of the Self. Bondage refers to the sense of, and identification with, the limitations of body, mind, intellect, and time, space, object. We are ever free, but are only deluded that we are bound in the cycle of birth and death. Self-realisation, or mokṣa, can be attained while living in the world (jīvanmukti), upon departure from the gross body (videhamukti), or in stages after leaving the gross body (kramamukti). For further study, see Ādi Śaṅkarācārya's *Vivekacūḍāmaṇi*.

64. What causes an individual to consider himself bound?

Avidyā (ignorance) is the cause. Ignorance of one's true nature results in the false sense of separateness, incompleteness, and limitation. Avidyā expresses itself as the three guṇas and results in identification with the body, mind, and intellect, which leads the individual to believe that he is limited and bound by time, space, and object.

Example: Due to ignorance, I identify myself with the misconceptions that I am limited in knowledge, that I am born and therefore will die, and that I need other things or beings to be happy. Such identification and sense of individuality is bondage. Non-recognition of my true nature (non-apprehension) leads to the superimposition or imagination of who I am (misapprehension).

65. How can the knowledge of the Self be imparted if the Self is not an object?

The Guru, in keeping with the śāstras (scriptures), adopts a peculiar methodology of teaching, wherein he uses the twofold process of anvaya-vyatireka (the principle of variable-invariable or inclusion-exclusion) and adhyāropa apavāda (the principle of deliberate superimposition-negation) to indicate to the disciple his true nature, the Truth behind the declaration of the Upaniṣad, Tat tvam asi, 'That thou art.'

- Anvaya, or the variable factor, revealing the nature of tvam, 'you': The identification of Consciousness with the body, mind, and intellect provides us with experiences strong enough for us to conclude that the

'I' in us is the body, mind, and intellect. When we say, 'I am thin', or 'I am agitated', or 'I am intelligent,' the respective variable factors are the body, mind, and intellect by which we feel we have been conditioned.

- Vyatireka, or the invariable factor, revealing the nature of Tat, 'That': The invariable factor is the very core of our being, pure Consciousness, which is aware of all the variable factors, but is unaffected by them. When seen from the standpoint of creation, the variable factors of birth, sustenance, and death take place in the presence of the one invariable source behind the cycle of creation.

Thus, the goal is to differentiate between the variable and invariable, and disidentify with the variable so that the invariable alone is revealed as one's true Self.

- Adhyāropa, or deliberate superimposition: The Guru and the scriptures initially give a seeming reality to the ignorant notions that we entertain, without negating them, such as our notions of 'I' and the relative world.

- Apavāda, or the subsequent negation: Once ignorance is recognised as the cause of the I-notion and the world, and these notions are negated, the Self reveals.

Example: As children, we are taught that the sky is blue (adhyāropa). Later, we are taught that the sky does not actually have any colour (apavāda). So too, we initially study in depth about jīva-jagat-Īśvara, the law of karma, and so on. (adhyāropa). Later, we learn that all differentiation and sense of separateness is to be negated (apavāda) because Brahman (Oneness) alone is.

66. What is the difference between self-hypnotism and Self-realisation?

All hypnotic effects are temporary; realisation of the eternal Self is not. The process of meditation can be considered as dehypnotising ourselves from our attachments and identifications. This process leads to the final rediscovery of the unconditioned Self.

67. What are the three direct means of knowledge for Self-realisation?

According to Vedānta, the three direct means of knowledge that help the seeker attain Self-realisation are:

- Śravaṇa: Listening to spiritual teachings with faith and reverence.
- Manana: Based on our śravaṇa, logical reflection on, and clarification of, all doubts.
- Nididhyāsana: Contemplation in order to arrive at a firm conviction and live according to it.

All other spiritual practices – chanting, worship, pilgrimages, service, and so on – help purify and channel the mind, and are the indirect means of knowledge for Self-realisation.

68. What is meditation?

Meditation, in its subtlest import in advaita Vedānta, refers to the state of pure Consciousness, where the duality of subject and object, the triad of experiencer, experiencing, and the experienced, and the plurality of time, space, and object do not exist. Meditation is seen as the ultimate goal: Self-awareness.

Meditation is also commonly used today as a verb. It is often understood as a mere relaxation exercise; however, it has a deeper significance for sincere spiritual seekers who practise meditation as the contemplative means to attain Self-realisation. In the case of a seeker, meditation refers to the conscious process of quietening the mind to ultimately know, and abide in, the Self.

Other Sanskrit terms used for this process are dhāraṇā, dhyāna, samādhi (see Question 71). Swami Chinmayananda, in his text *Meditation & Life*, states: 'When the mind's thoughts have been nourished by study, and rendered quiet and peaceful by japa, to rest the hushed mind at the altar of the Self in a thrilled mood of choiceless contemplation, is meditation (dhyāna).' For further study, see *Meditation & Life* and *Art of Contemplation* by Swami Chinmayananda, and *Meditation: A Vision* by Swami Tejomayananda.

69. How many kinds of votaries are there among those who seek God?

Lord Kṛṣṇa names four types of votaries (people who turn to God) in *Gītā* Chapter 7.16:

- Ārta: A person in distress.
- Arthārthī: A person seeking wealth and worldly possessions.
- Jijñāsu: A person seeking higher Knowledge.
- Jñānī: A person of wisdom (who turns to God in pure love, not seeking anything).

70. Who is a yogī?

The word yogī comes from the root yuj, which means 'to unite.' He who has dissolved his lower self in the higher Self, that is, merged his individual consciousness with the universal Consciousness, is a yogī. The spiritual seeker becomes a yogī by first understanding the nature of the Self and then practising various disciplines to realise the Self.

71. What are the prescribed paths to reach the stage of a yogī?

There are many prescribed paths, all leading to the same goal: the path of knowledge (jñāna-yoga), the path of devotion (bhakti-yoga), and the path of service or dedicated action (karma-yoga). Additionally, the path of rāja-yoga or aṣṭāṅga-yoga is exhaustively described in the yoga aphorisms of Sage Patañjali. The 'eight limbs' of aṣṭāṅga-yoga are the eight steps to Self-realisation:

- Yama: Ahiṁsā (non-violence in thought, word, and deed), satya (truthfulness), asteya (not stealing), brahmacarya (celibacy or self-control), and aparigraha (not aggrandising or hoarding).

- Niyama: Śauca (purity of body and mind), santoṣa (contentment), tapa (penance or sacrifice for a higher goal), svādhyāya (self-study), and Īśvara-praṇidhāna (surrender and dedication to God).

- Āsana: Postures conducive to purifying and balancing energy channels in the body and mind.

- Prāṇāyāma: Control of the prāṇika forces (systematic breathing is only a part of these forces; see Question 52).

- Pratyāhāra: Restraining the senses; withdrawing the senses from their respective objects.

- Dhāraṇā: Steadying the mind.

- Dhyāna: Contemplation.

- Samādhi: Direct experience of the state of infinite Bliss.

For further study on yoga, see The *Holy Gītā* by Swami Chinmayananda. For further study on samādhi, including savikalpa and nirvikalpa samādhi, see Swami Chinmayananda's commentary on *Vivekacūḍāmaṇi* by Ādi Śaṅkara.

72. Who is a Guru?

Gu represents darkness, or ignorance of the highest Reality, and ru represents removal of that ignorance. Thus, the Guru is one who removes the disciple's ignorance and allows the Truth to be revealed.

In *Vivekacūḍāmaṇi,* Ādi Śaṅkara describes the Guru as 'he who is well versed in the scriptures, sinless, not afflicted by desires, knower of the Supreme, calm as the fire that has burnt up its fuel, a boundless ocean of mercy that needs no cause to express, and an intimate friend to those who have surrendered unto him.'

Vedānta teaches that the Guru, who is one with God, or Brahman, is not just a physical entity. He is the ever-present, inner guiding force within every seeker. Thus, the Guru's physical or subtle form manifests as needed solely for the benefit of the disciple.

73. Who is a disciple?

A disciple (śiṣya) is one who subjects himself to the Guru's discipline. A disciple is one who is devoted to the Guru, implicitly follows the Guru's teachings, and serves the Guru for the sole purpose of enlightenment. The Guru guides the disciple as needed, to progress on his spiritual journey, to go beyond saṁsāra (the cycle of birth and death) and attain Self-realisation.

The spiritual relationship between a Guru and a śiṣya is similar to that of a parent and a child. Parents give the child life, but the Guru gives the disciple freedom from life and death by guiding him to realise his own true nature. Thus, the disciple can never repay the Guru for this debt.

74. What are the qualifications of a spiritual seeker?

Sādhana catuṣṭaya is the set of four qualifications to be developed by a sincere seeker in order to study Vedānta and realise the Self. The four qualifications are: viveka, vairāgya, śamādi-ṣaṭ-sampatti and mumukṣutva.

- Viveka: nitya-anitya-vastu vivekaḥ, 'discrimination between the Eternal and the ephemeral;' a firm conviction of the mind that Brahman alone is real (unchanging) and the universe of names and forms is unreal (changing).

- Vairāgya: iha-amutra-phala-bhoga-virāgaḥ, 'non-attachment to the fruits of one's actions in this life or next;' leads one to renounce cravings for transitory enjoyments.

- Śamādi-ṣaṭ-sampatti: 'the six-fold wealth [attributes to be cultivated], beginning with śama,':

    - Śama: Control over the mind; detaching the mind from sense objects (not allowing sense objects to enter the mind).

    - Dama: Control over the sense organs; withdrawing the senses from sense objects (not allowing the sense organs to go out to the sense objects).

    - Uparati or uparama: Inner withdrawal, where the mind is no longer affected by the external world of objects.

- Titikṣā: Forbearance; patiently persevering in the face of all afflictions and difficulties, without grievance or worry.

- Śraddhā: Faith; firm conviction in the Guru, Lord, scriptures, and Self.

- Samādhāna: Single pointedness in scriptural studies, reflection, and contemplation.

• Mumukṣutva: 'Intense yearning for Liberation' from all bondage; longing for freedom from identification with the three instruments (body, mind, and intellect), the three states (waking, dream, and deep sleep) and the three limitations (time, space, and object).

Ādi Śaṅkara says in *Vivekacūḍāmaṇi*, 'He who has a keen memory, enough knowledge of the world outside, an understanding of the world within, who believes in and stands up for the scriptures and can refute arguments against them – such a one is fit for receiving Ātma-vidyā (Self-knowledge, Brahma-vidyā)'.

An adhikārī is thus a qualified student who is fit to receive Brahma-vidyā from the Guru. Such a person:

• Has general knowledge of the Vedas and similar scriptures.

• Has a pure mind.

• Is endowed with sādhana catuṣṭaya.

- Performs nitya karmas (daily duties) and naimittika karmas (special duties).
- Avoids kāmya karmas (desire-born actions) and niṣiddha karmas (wrongful actions).
- Observes prāyaścitta karmas (acts of penance to correct or improve himself) when necessary.

* Fasting from activity in which you've been indulgent

PART FIVE
WHY RELIGION?

PART FIVE:
WHY RELIGION?

75. Why does religion seem to appeal only to the minority?

As long as the majority of humankind searches for happiness and freedom on the physical plane, religion will appeal only to the minority. With the development of his mental and intellectual faculties, the aspirant's spirit of inquiry grows. Religion provides such an inquiring mind with the highest goal of life and the paths to reach it. For those who are at the sensual level and have not yet outgrown their baser tendencies, religion will not have an immediate appeal.

76. What is meant by the statement, 'Hinduism is tolerant'?

Dr. S. Radhakrishnan (former President of India) said, "Hinduism is wholly free from the strange obsession that the acceptance of a particular religious metaphysic is necessary for salvation and non-acceptance thereof is a heinous sin meriting eternal punishment in hell. Hindus do not lay exclusive claims to salvation, and they do not believe that God will be pleased by the wholesale slaughter of those of His creatures whose beliefs are mistaken".

77. What is the relationship between science and religion?

Science and religion are interrelated, so when either disowns the other, there is decay in society. In order to establish harmony, society should embrace both science and religion.

Objective science presents a view of life through the study of the constantly changing world. But the human being cannot achieve complete happiness through scientific advancements alone. Subjective science, or spirituality, presents a way of life through the introspective study of the unchanging Reality and the means to attain that Reality. Spirituality, Vedānta in particular, teaches fundamental values and their practical applications in order to achieve the goal of complete and permanent happiness.

Science raises the standard of living, whereas religion raises the standard of life. Science and religion can vitalise each other. Material advancement through scientific methods will be fruitless without the nobler values of healthy living that religion teaches. Just as mere knowledge of architecture and a perfect blueprint cannot, without good quality materials, create a strong structure, so too, a materially advanced society that does not adhere to value based living cannot truly progress. Man can attain great heights by recognising the real worth and utility of both science and religion.

78. How do we discover why God created this world?

One can look at this question in different ways:

- Even in scientific investigations, the 'why' remains unanswered (why the sun, why gravity, and so on). When it comes to nature's laws, motive hunting is beyond the realm of science. This question should be asked to God, for He alone can answer it fully.

- On the path of sādhanā, when the mind's impurities have been removed and māyā has been transcended, the Truth will be revealed and all questions and doubts will be cleared.
- To attain the state of Oneness, the entire triad of the questioner (ego), questioning, and the questioned must dissolve. In Oneness, who questions whom?
- Because the world is constantly changing, it cannot be defined as 'real.' How can we ask why the world was created when the created world is but an illusion? When the equipments of experience are transcended, the projected world merges into the One and there is no world to be questioned.

79. How does Vedānta help a person achieve happiness?

An individual's life is a continuity of experiences, driven by a constant yearning to achieve complete and lasting happiness, a fuller and deeper peace. To live harmoniously, one must have a right understanding of oneself and the world.

Vedānta does not teach indifference to sorrow, poverty, injustice, and so on, but does teach how wrong estimation of the world and superimposition of false values on things, beings, and situations can result in unhappy and painful experiences. Vedānta teaches one how to readjust one's view of, and relationship with, the world, in order to ultimately realise the Self.

PART SIX

QUESTIONS AND ANSWERS WITH SWAMI CHINMAYANANDA

PART SIX:
QUESTIONS AND ANSWERS WITH SWAMI CHINMAYANANDA

Excerpts from a questionnaire by Bharatiya Vidya Bhavan
(circa 1975)

80. Is the influence of religion on the masses declining? If not, how can we account for corruption and other such pointers that indicate widespread deterioration in ethical and moral values?

All those who have eyes can vividly see that religion in India is today more popular than ever before. Famous temples are overflowing with pilgrims; new temples are mushrooming all over; temple construction committees are spontaneously rising up even in the most distant corners of shy villages, and they are sincerely struggling to find funds and materials for rebuilding and renovating the neglected and dilapidated old shrines.

Daily newspapers all over the country are announcing in their columns dozens of spiritual talks and religious functions. Religion is rampant as never before. This is, to an extent, true all over the world. The widespread sense of insecurity, political and economic, compels the human being to run to religion, to use it perhaps as a crutch.

Honestly, I do not believe that most of the immorality and corruption found in the world is caused by any lack of religion. Immorality and corruption are, at best, the by-products of unintelligent laws, general scarcity, rise in population, and the consequent unnatural, crowded living conditions in impossibly large metropolitan centers. And certainly in India, the sudden change in our values, brought about by the spirit of secularism, is also nibbling away at the confused hearts of the illiterate and uneducated. If we can lace this freshly streaming spirit of religion in our country with at least a dash of deeper philosophical and cultural depth, a bigger change in the moral flavour of our social life will surely follow.

81. The traditional charge against Hinduism is that it is fatalistic and that it inhibits progress by making people slaves to the belief in the inevitability of whatever is to happen. How far is this true? What is the basis of such an accusation, which is being advanced even today by well-meaning and highly educated people?

The idea of destiny is very much a part of Hinduism, and as a truth, it cannot be denied. The subtle thinkers, our ṛṣis, while analysing and studying life in the raw, in the light of their own subjective experiences of the spiritual Essence, came to the honest conclusion that there is an inevitable continuity in all happenings. The present is naturally a product of the entire past. Therefore, the past orders, controls, and governs the present. 'This is destiny!' cry all hasty students.

This hasty conclusion is what the Western missionaries have gathered from their 'hurry-burry' studies of our deep and profound thought. They translated and criticised. And these criticisms are available in well bound, attractive volumes at many universities and public libraries. The modern, educated Indian reads these books. The thoughtful reader gets shocked by the conflicts therein, but the thoughtless reader comes to blindly believe all that he gathers from these incompetent, second hand, smothered ideas. The hasty Western student understands only half of our law of karma, and those who misunderstand it preach the hopeless philosophy of 'destiny' as being the essence of Hindu thought.

'The present is the product of the past' is not all that the law of karma declares. Half a thought in any philosophy can become a dangerous, false statement. The law of karma, when completely declared, insists upon a scientifically unassailable truth: 'The present is the product of the past, and the future is the past modified in the present.' The present with reference to the past is already 'destiny,' but by the very texture of our present thoughts and by the quality of our present actions – self-effort – we are ordering and building our future. This larger implication is an organic part of the law of karma and cannot ever be separated without destroying the truth of the entire concept. In short, what we meet in life is 'destiny' (prārabdha) and how we meet what we meet in life is self-effort (puruṣārtha).

The present criticism that 'it [destiny] inhibits progress by making people slaves to the belief in the inevitability of whatever is to happen' cannot stand in the light of any deep inquiry. The present is ordered by the past; therefore, the present is inevitable. In the forenoon, I consume a lot of salt; in the afternoon, it is inevitable that I will feel thirsty. It is sheer wisdom to recognise the present as the effect of some cause or causes initiated in the past. Wisdom is the antidote for all confusion and the solace for all fear.

Historically the Hindus would not have survived as a cultural unit after all these centuries of persecution and political slavery but for this deep understanding and their consequent unshakeable heroism and inner composure in the face of all their trials. Maybe we must now re-educate the public in the positive aspect of the law of karma: that thought by thought and action by action, we are sculpting our future.

82. **It is said that the greatest strength of Hinduism is its breadth of outlook and that this is also its greatest weakness, in that there are very few common prescribed religious observances obligatory for all, as in other religions. Is it necessary and possible to outline certain basic, minimum observances for all Hindus?**

This is a very delicate and sensitive area, and no one should dash into it with any hasty remedy. Hinduism is geared toward producing saints, evolving sages, and raising Masters.

Spiritual perfection in the individual is the goal. Beautifying the mind, uplifting the vision to the Highest, and thereby coming to manifest the glory of the flame of Existence, so as to enrich and enthrall the world around him – this is an art. And indeed, art can grow only in freedom.

Religions, at their lower levels, aim at organising society and harnessing the emotional fervour of the population, thus generating a kind of social militancy, which is, no doubt, good for the political and economic well-being of a community. However, the sorrows that such a society can spawn are indeed calamitous. The pages of human history may have been cleaner if not for such religions and their deadly fanaticisms. Whether it is the Christian War of the Roses and other bloody battles waged, or the Islamic jihādas, or the Śaivite and Vaiṣnavite conflicts in the South, or the feuds between the Ārya Samājīs and the Sanātanīs in the North – every one of them is an example of the confrontations that inevitably arise when religions are organised and religious thought is walled in by dogma and rituals.

I am not against organisation. I am very much conscious that I myself am the head of an organisation with a vision, and this organisation is growing every day as a result of my personal, tireless endeavours. Organisation is unavoidably needed. We need churches, mosques, temples, and other such institutions. Large masses of people congregating therein, can thereby develop in their actions and thoughts a rhythm at once loving and divine. But in prescribing these strict religious schemes of service, we must grow truly sensitive to feel how far we should go and not become insistent. Otherwise, we will destroy the spontaneity in the seeker, which many other religions do. Those who no longer need the warm protection of a religious institution must be able to walk out of its motherly embrace and seek their own independent and fuller expressions in the quest divine.

I believe the present system is more than sufficient for this purpose. All that we need is a team of intelligent, educated interpreters who can update the truths of our philosophy and religious texts to fit the thought patterns of our own times. If the long term plan is to train such a cadre of priests, then, as a short term policy, I would strongly recommend that such literature, in the form of pamphlets, be distributed to the masses through the temples, as a part of the usual prasāda, especially on sacred days and festive occasions.

83. Will the fundamental values of Hinduism be in any way affected by the eradication of casteism, toward which a concerted effort is being made now at all levels? If harijanas, who constitute a sizable population among Hindus, are made to feel that their religion exposes them to ridicule, how are they to love that religion? In other words, how can all sections of Hindus be made to take equal interest in, and have the same sense of belonging to, their religion?

'Casteism' has no place in Hinduism. The word 'caste' indicates a scientific classification of man's inner personality, which is universal and true for all times. Every one of us expresses in one of three distinct moods (sattva, rajas, tamas) due to the preponderance of one over the other two. Based on these moods, the human mind functions in four different grades (varṇas). These psychological classifications are called castes. In fact, caste only shows how you are cast.

When a thought, however good it may be, is with an individual for a long period of time, his vested interests come to abuse it, and the distorted thought, in time, often grows to become an ugly veil in society. Casteism is not permitted, while castes are inevitable. There are brāhmaṇas (Brahmins) in America as much as śūdras in Rome. Where in the world can you not find honest, ethical, clean thinkers (brāhmaṇas); enthusiastic and tireless leaders of men in the political field (kṣatriyas); commercial men (vaiśyas); and labour oriented persons (śūdras)? But not to recognise that they are all different aspects of the one infinite Lord is a pernicious conspiracy brought into society by the covetous. Such things happen around the world when leaders try to guard their own selfish interests. The sad and unjust condition of the African-Americans in America is a case in point. Theirs is but a history of 200 years. The evil that we [in India] are faced with has a history of about 3,000 years.

Yet, in our [India's] 30 years of independence, we have, in our Constitution, updated the rights and privileges of the harijanas to be at par with the brāhmaṇas. True, the emotional integration is not yet complete, especially in the interior conservative villages. But the progress that we have already made is phenomenal. We shall continue the same policy, and perhaps we must intelligently modulate it to bring about some more self-respect and self-sufficiency in the younger generation, which has already been redeemed. They [the younger generation] should not lean too much on the government or play an endless tune of complaints. It is time that they show their political responsibility and social maturity. Now they are flooding into schools and colleges. If we can end, through our education system, our political attitude of strict untouchability and unapproachability toward our cultural traditions and religious literature, we could perhaps re-educate our brothers much quicker. They have suffered in neglect not because there was any scriptural sanction for it, but because of an error in reading and interpreting the pregnant [scriptural] statements, or perhaps even because of a deliberate act of political manoeuvering by those who were then in power wanting to protect and perpetuate their vested interests.

84. Hinduism has always renewed or revitalised itself according to the needs of the times. In today's context, are any corrective measures called for? If so, who will bring them about, and how can they be brought about and made acceptable to the masses?

When a culture is alive, it will create its own answers to all the insistent demands of the historical period and the evils of that period. Our culture has done it many a time in the past. Vyāsa, Buddha, Śaṅkara, Rāmānuja, Madhvācārya, Vivekananda and Nārāyaṇa Guru, are but a few examples. In the same way, the new age will create its own Masters.

When we look around, we see that this rejuvenation is being accomplished all over again. The stupendous activities of pioneers like Swami Sivananda, Aurobindo, Ramana Maharṣi, Swami Rama Das of Kanjangad, Neem Karoli Baba, and others; the gigantic efforts of Śrī Satya Sai Baba; the benign services of institutions like Bharatiya Vidya Bhavan, Gita Press of Gorakhpur, and others; [all these] like the organised, disciplined, and intelligently manoeuvered programs of Chinmaya Mission, now spread all over the country and abroad. These are answers to the 'throb' that is now being felt within our Hindu community. To say that Hinduism has not shown any response to the needs of our times is to be utterly blind to what is happening today not only in our country, but all around the world.

The emphasis is slowly shifting from ritualism to yoga and a deeper study of philosophy, [to prepare one] to enter into and explore the secrets of inner life through contemplation and meditation. To run schools and colleges in a general atmosphere of culture and religion, to give our growing generation a fair chance to judge for itself its own traditions and culture, to provide educated preachers who can preach religious and spiritual ideas with reference to our immediate social and economic needs, to spare some time on the air and space in the newspapers and journals to discuss constructively the practical ideas of *Bhagavad-gītā,* to revive through attractive programs people's enthusiasm to reach our temples for mass silent prayers – these are some of the programs I would strongly recommend, since these are the very programs I have been working on, indeed, very successfully, for many years.

85. Are fasting and such other dietary regulations necessary for leading a spiritual life? Is a Guru essential for one to enter the spiritual path and attain the goal?

To withdraw the mind's wandering attention from the outer world of names and forms, and to redirect its attention steadily to the spring of all activities in one's own within, is spiritual seeking. To center our attention on this inner silence and tranquility, and to confront the world of happenings around, is spiritual life. Naturally, therefore, fasting becomes important, not necessarily as the not-eating of food, which we take in by the mouth, but as a strict discipline maintained in all our intakes – seeing, hearing, smelling, touching, even feeling and thinking.

The very fact that you are asking these questions clearly shows that we need teachers to teach us. Think for a moment: is there anything that we do well today, with confidence or some amount of mastery, which has not been taught to us? If, for every perfect act in the world, in any department of activity, by anyone, we need the guidance of an instructor, then you can very well understand the need for a Guru on the spiritual path, where we have to deal with the subtlest forces and the enormous confusions of the vehicle called the mind, and its moods called delusions.

86. Will mantras lose their sanctity if they are not chanted in Sanskrit? There are various saṁskāras prescribed in Hinduism from birth to death. Many of these saṁskāras are not being observed today. Should they not be revived?

Mantras are not mere words. That which uplifts us when we reflect on it is a mantra. So the sound symbol, or mantra, serves as the rails for the train of thought to smoke through and reach its destination of vivid and direct experience. Whatever be the language in which mantras are chanted, each individual will reflect upon them in his own native language. Thus, when an American chants Śivoham, he cannot reflect upon the significance of this mantra except in his own native tongue: 'I am auspiciousness; I am Śiva.' Therefore, what harm can there be in his mantra being in any language?

No doubt, Sanskrit is such a perfect language that the very vibrations of the words in the mantra have a soothing effect on the mind. Yet, this is but a very superficial gain as compared to the deep significance, divine glory, endless richness, fabulous beauty – the holiness and preciousness – of the meaning arrived at through reflection. Will anyone ever purchase a costly pearl necklace in order to have only its velvet container?

For the masses, celebrations and demonstrations have an impressive impact. Even a peace loving country like ours must have military parades on Republic Day in order to reinforce the confidence of the masses in the might of the country. These saṁskāras (rituals) have an effect, just as convocation assemblies, marriage ceremonies, the laying of foundation stones, the unveiling of statues and the inaugurations of dams, and so on, do. Saṁskāras, if conducted by all, should bring about a sense of discipline and a pride of belonging, providing a healthy reminder of the significant cultural meanings of these rituals to all those who attend such functions.

87. What is the role of rituals in religion? Are they to be discouraged?

Rituals are objective dramatisations of the subjective art of self-perfection; such ceremonious and attractive displays of rhythm and beauty cannot be eliminated from human life. Historically, it is true that whenever ritualism is removed, churches, mosques, and temples are closed down and replaced by military parades, nightclubs and their excesses, racecourse crowds, boxing galleries, and other announcement centres. Let the public decide what they want. I would prefer that my countrymen have religious rituals entertaining them rather than the more dangerous and immoral alternatives.

88. What is your view regarding proselytisation? If you were convinced that Hinduism has a great role to play in the world, would you consider proselytisation?

Proselytising is the cheap commercialism of religion. It is not sanctioned in Hinduism. We are enjoined only to propagate the spiritual science that is our inheritance. By gathering an understanding of the Hindu Upaniṣads and gaining a glimpse of the universal thoughts expounded by the ṛṣis therein, a Christian can perhaps become a better Christian, a Hindu surely a better Hindu. Such training gives the human mind a subtler vision to see clearly the eternal thoughts expounded by the spiritual Masters and the silent content in their pregnant words.

Any individual must be welcomed into the fold of any faith to participate in its spiritual practices. But to convert the people as though they are manufactured goods to be stamped with trademarks and packed and stored away in churches, temples, or mosques is a repugnant idea, choking the very spirit of Hindu scientific thought. However, we have every right to receive our brothers back – Hindus who had, because of their own confusions or due to some cruel political and/or economic pressures, left us to embrace other faiths. This is not conversion. This is a return into the fold of those who lost their way and strayed for a time.

89. Are changes visible in Hinduism's doctrines and in the modes of individual and collective worship as a result of contact with the West?

Visible changes are recognisable in other faiths due to their contacts with Hinduism. Evidently, today Hinduism is shedding her light and imparting her fragrance to Western thought. And I must say that the reverse is not at all visible or true. The scientific thoughts of the West have recently confirmed our japa technique and the powers inherent in the bīja-akṣaras (sacred syllables, mantras). This is the contribution of the transcendental meditation techniques of Mahesh Yogi; this elementary technique of japa in Hinduism has become the great transcendental meditation so popular in the West today.

The Christian authorities have started emphasising more than ever the need for meditation. They are re-reading their Bible and discovering a sanction for yoga in the words of Jesus. It is not too infrequent nowadays to see church programs that include yoga practices. I am indicating these only to demonstrate the spectacular signs of Hindu influence now glaringly evident in the West. In short, Hinduism gave more in her casual trip to the West than what she herself accepted when she suffered the embrace of the West all these centuries.

And is it not true that Christianity in India has become more Hinduised? Is not Mother Mary now wearing a sārī? Don't we hear the sounds of cymbals from churches? Don't churches now smell more of incense? Don't we see oil lamps replacing candles? Are processions, with Indian drums, of Jesus on elephants not a common sight in India? Are not Christian priests now calling themselves svāmīs? Are not their monasteries now becoming āśramas? Have not even churches started being called temples? Is it not becoming fashionable now to have a Hindu name for every Thomas, John, Mary, and Anna?

I do not think Hinduism has anything to gain from the West. . . . We have much to give them. . . . They are taking. . . . And they must take more.

Hari Om

APPENDIX

Hindu scriptural literature is so vast and comprehensive that there is no branch of knowledge left uninvestigated by the great seers of India. The Hindu was never satisfied unless every question that he faced – be it material, scientific, religious, philosophical or spiritual – was thoroughly discussed in all aspects to its irrefutable conclusion.

The lists and tables that follow will give insight into the progress of Indian thought through the ages, and will show how our forefathers relentlessly investigated the various fields of knowledge; discovered scientific, philosophical, and spiritual truths; enunciated and codified them in systematic treatises on various subjects; and bequeathed them to posterity. To them, Sanātana-dharma meant the eternal values of life that they adhered to in all circumstances. For them, Hinduism was not a closed book, because in their profound wisdom, they recognised the fact that there is no limit to knowledge. Search. You will find. The more you search, the more you will find.

Swami Chinmayananda

VEDAS

1. *Ṛg (Ṛk)-veda:* 432,000 Saṁhitās; 28 Brāhmaṇas; 42 Upaniṣads; total of 707,000 stanzas.

2. *Yajur-veda:* 250,000 Saṁhitās; 32 Brāhmaṇas; 60 Upaniṣads; total of 455,000 stanzas.

3. *Sāma-veda:* 600,000 Saṁhitās; 21 Brāhmaṇas; 90 Upaniṣads; total of 950,000 stanzas.

4. *Atharva-veda:* 300,000 Saṁhitās; 11 Brāhmaṇas; 52 Upaniṣads; total of 480,000 stanzas.

UPA-VEDAS

1. *Āyurveda: Cakrānuveśa* by Sanaka; original works attributed to Dhanvantarī, extant works by Caraka, Suśruta, and Vegabha (also a bacteriologist); the science of longevity.

2. *Dhanurveda: Praveśāṣṭa-prakāśam* by Pracetas; original works attributed to Bhṛgu and Viśvāmitra; the science of warfare.

3. *Gandharva-veda: Svarānuvāda* by Nārada; the science of music.

4. *Sthāpatya-veda: Siddhāntopanyastha* by Aśvini Kumāras; the science of architecture.

DARŚANAS: SCHOOLS OF PHILOSOPHY

1. **Nyāya:** Svayambhū's *Prabhāntarīkṣa*, Sage Gautama's *Nyāya Sūtras*, *Tarka-saṅgraha*, Bhāṣa-pariccheda, *Siddhānta-muktāvali*; *Kusumāñjali* by Udāyanācārya is an important work on this subject.

2. **Vaiśeṣika:** Kratu's *Darśanānubhava*; subsequent work by Ṛṣi Kaṇāda.

3. **Sāṅkhya:** Original work is Mārīca's *Anubhava*; subsequent authoritative work by Sage Kapila.

4. **Yoga:** Original treatise by Cyamana called *Vṛthyājitharṇava*; subsequent works by Sage Patañjali, with elaborate commentaries by Bhoja Deva, Vācaspati Miśra, Vijñāna Bhikṣu, and Nāgoji Bhatta.

5. **Mīmāṁsā:** Original work *Arthaprakāśa* of Ṛṣi Aṅgirasa; subsequent work by Sage Jaimini; also called *Pūrva Mīmāṁsā* or *Karma Mīmāṁsā.*

6. **Vedānta:** Also called *Uttara Mīmāṁsā*; original work is said to be Lord Brahmā's *Prahīkṣa-pradīpa*; subsequent work is *Brahmasūtras* by Vedavyāsa.

ŚABDA-ŚĀSTRAS

1. Śikṣā: Phonetics

Maheśvara's *Śikṣā* and *Nārada Bhāṣya* are also called *prātisākhyas* totalling 172,000 stanzas. This subject is also dealt with in a chapter in *Taittirīya Āraṇyaka* and a book called *Māṇḍukī Śikṣā.*

2. Kalpa: Design and Construction of Religious Sites

Devi's *Vyavasthānubhava* is the original treatise of 248,000 stanzas. Subsequently, several works on this subject came out of each of the four Vedas. Examples include:

- From *Ṛg-veda: Aśvalāyana, Śaṅkhāyana, Śaunaka.*
- From *Sāma-veda: Masaka, Lātyāyana, Drahyāyana*
- From *Yajur-veda: Āpastamba, Satyāṣaḍha, Hiraṇyakeśi, Mānava, Bharadvāja, Vathūla, Vyākhanāśa, Maitra, Kathā, Varāha* and so on. (from *Kṛṣṇa Yajur-veda), Kātyāyana* (from *Śukla Yajur-veda*).
- From *Atharva-veda: Kauśitaka.*

3. Vyākaraṇa: Grammar

First came the *Maheśvara Sūtras* and *Nārada Bhāṣya,* totaling 100,000 stanzas. Thereafter came the *Pāṇinī Sūtras*

(*Aṣṭādhyāyī*, the world-renowned grammatical work that remains unparalleled to date and is accepted as such by Western scholars also) and Patañjali's *Mahābhāṣya*, both of which are important and authoritative treatises.

There were other notable grammarians before Pāṇinī, namely, Apiśali, Kaśyapa, Gārgya, Gālava, Cakravarman, Bharadvāja, Śakaṭāyana, Sakālya, Senaka, and Sphoṭāyana. Kātyāyana was an outstanding grammarian after Pāṇinī.

4. Nirukta: Vaidika Etymology

Gaṇeśa's *Nirukta* and Śeṣa's *Bhāṣya* comprise 55,000 stanzas. Subsequent work was done by Yāskācārya. A well-known work is *Amara Koṣa*, also known as *Nāma-liṅga-anuśāsanam*, written by the world's first lexicographer, Amarasiṁha, a great scholar who flourished in the court of King Vikramāditya and who was a contemporary of the great poet Kālidāsa.

5. Chandas: Prosody (Metre)

Viṣṇu's *Chandorṇava* is comprised of 172,000 stanzas. The subsequent work of *Chanda Śāstra* came from Piṅgala. Many other works came later, including *Nidāna Sūtra*, *Shruta-bodha*, *Vāṇībhūṣaṇa*, *Vṛtta-darpaṇa*, *Vṛtta-ratnākara*, *Vṛtta-kaumudī*, *Chandomañjarī*, and *Savṛtha-tilaka*. *Chandomañjarī* by Gaṅgādāsa is an important work on this subject.

The number of metres possible in Sanskrit poetry is an astronomical figure. The word for metre in Sanskrit is vṛtta. There are three types of vṛttas: sama vṛtta, viṣama vṛtta, and ardha-sama vṛtta. The categorisation depends on whether the composition of each line in a four line stanza is the same or different. For example, in sama vṛttas, the maximum number of letters in a line is 26. With 1-26 hard sound (guru) and soft sound (laghu) letters in each line, the maximum number of metre permutations under sama vṛtta is 87,108,864.

6. Jyotiṣa: Astronomy and Astrology

Sūrya's *Brihadāṅka-pradīpa* has 100,000 stanzas. The subsequent important works are Āryabhaṭṭīya by Āryabhaṭṭa and *Sūrya Siddhānta* by Bhāskarācārya. There are also treatises on the subject by Varāha Mihira, Gārga, and Brahmagupta.

ARTS AND SCIENCES

1. *Akṣara Lakṣa*: Attributed to Sage Vālmīki; deals with the branches of mathematics: arithmetic, algebra, geometry, trigonometry, physics and applied mathematics; consists of 50 chapters; acknowledges the earlier discoveries of Hanumāna, Jaimini, Brihaspati, Kaśyapa; also deals with geography, air/wind, electricity, mineralogy, and more.

2. *Artha Śāstra*: Short treatise attributed to Sage Vyāsa, wherein he deals with more than 80 ways of earning wealth through dhārmika means; extant work attributed to Kauṭilya.

3. *Citra Karma*: Believed to have been authored by Bhīma; deals with the science of fine arts; 12 chapters with more than 200 sketches; explains a novel method by which an artist can create the complete figure of a person after having seen only a portion of his body.

4. *Dhātu Vāda*: Believed to have been written by Aśvini Kumāras; deals with the science of alchemy and the conversion of baser metals into gold; a treatise on dhātus, or primary substances, and their reactions and combinations.

5. *Gaja Śāstra*: Attributed to Kumārasvāmī; deals with the behaviour and characteristics of elephants; gives methodology to categorise elephants on the basis of certain body marks.

6. *Kāla Nirṇaya*: Attributed to Lord Kārtikeya; deals with the concept of time, auspicious and inauspicious occasions, limitations of time and its measurements, and the presiding deities of various dates, constellations, and so on.

7. *Lakṣaṇa Śāstra*: Attributed to Sage Śakaṭāyana; deals with the determination of gender in both animate and inanimate creation; Babhru Muni's work *Kanyā Lakṣaṇa* lists characteristics of an unwed girl that can be used to reveal her future, family life, children, prosperity, chastity, and so on.

8. *Śakuna Śāstra*: Sage Gārga's detailed treatise on omens or indications of success and failure in endeavours.

9. *Mālinī Śāstra*: Attributed to Sage Ṛṣyaśruṅga; a comprehensive treatise dealing with flowers and their arrangements, including making garlands and bouquets, how women can adorn themselves with flowers, conveying messages of love through flowers, and so on.

10. *Malla Śāstra*: Attributed to Malla Muni; deals with health preservation and bodybuilding; the science of gymnastics, athletics, wrestling, and so on.

11. *Mahendra Jāla*: Attributed to Vīrabāhu; deals with the science of magic; describes the art of creating illusions (flying, walking on water, and so on).

12. *Parakāyā Praveśa*: Attributed to Vālakhilyas; deals with the eight siddhis – aṇimā, mahimā, laghimā, garimā, īśitva, vaśitva, prāpti and prākāśya; the 32 yogas leading to parakāyā praveśa or the transfer of one's jīva, at will, to another body (as was done by Ādi Śaṅkara into the body of King Amaruka).

13. *Ratna Parīkṣā and Kanaka Parīkṣā*: Attributed to Sage Vatsyana; deals with the science of testing precious stones and gold for genuineness, including the 24 lakṣanas (signs) of precious stones and gems, their categorisation, and the 32 tests of their quality and genuineness.

14. *Sāmudrika Śāstra*: Attributed to Samudra Rājā, or Lord Varuṇa; deals with the various body marks that are said to indicate a person's character, life, and experiences; said to have started with Varuṇa's reading of the auspicious marks on Lord Viṣṇu's reclining body; further developed through the later contributions of Nārada, Varāha, Māṇḍavya, and so on; one of its branches is palmistry.

15. *Saudāmini Śāstra*: Attributed to Sage Mātaṅga of Mount Ṛṣyamūka; deals with chāyā grahaṇa, or the power and use of shadows; also deals with the science of photography and its derivations.

16. ***Śabda Śāstra*:** Attributed to Ṛṣi Kaṇḍika; deals with sounds and echoes, their categorisations and modifications, and the mechanical reproduction of sounds (pitch, frequency, velocity, and so on).

17. ***Śakti Tantra Śāstra*:** Attributed to Sage Agastya; consists of eight detailed chapters that deal with the various energies and powers in the universe, including the 64 kinds of energy in nature; the sun, moon, and their śaktis; the practical applications to harness such forces; the unlimited energy contained in the atom; an atom's fusion and fission; and nuclear science.

18. ***Śilpa Śāstra*:** Attributed to Sage Kaśyapa; deals with sculpture, construction of idols, temples, palaces, and so on; 22 chapters with 307 categories of sculptures and over 100 types of images and idols, including their dimensions, proportions, and other characteristics; Viśvakarmā is said to have contributed much to the development of this science.

19. ***Sūpa Śāstra*:** Attributed to Sukeśa; deals with the science of cooking, which Sukeśa is said to have perfected to a science; contains various preparations of condiments, pickles, sweets, puddings, cakes; different dishes to suit the tastes of people in different parts of the world; sūpa means 'broth' (thus the word soup).

20. ***Turaṅga Śāstra*:** Comprehensive treatise on horses by Agnivarman; expounds on everything about horses, including breeding, upbringing, pedigree, points for

selection and various uses, including war; King Nala is also said to have written a treatise called *Aśva Hṛdaya* on this subject.

21. ***Vātāvaraṇa Śāstra***: Attributed to Sage Atri; deals with clouds, their categorisation and characteristics; 12 different kinds of rain; 64 types of lightning; 33 types of thunderbolts, and so on.

22. ***Viṣa Śāstra***: Attributed to the Aśvini Kumāras; exhaustive treatise on the science of poisons; elaborate discussions about the 32 broad categories of all poisons, including their properties, preparations, applications and antidotes.

23. ***Yantra Śāstra***: Attributed to Sage Bharadvāja; deals with the types of vehicles for movement on land, water, and air; also deals with the possibility and methodology of movement in space without any vehicle, using only mantras (mystic sound symbols) and tantras (energy forces).

PRAMĀṆAS: MEANS OF KNOWLEDGE

According to Hindu scriptures, the various means or sources of human knowledge are:

- **Pratyakṣa:** Perception.
- **Anumāna:** Inference.
- **Āpta Vākya (Śabda):** Testimony (verbal).
- **Upamāna:** Comparison.
- **Arthāpatti:** Postulation.
- **Anūpalabdhi:** Non-cognition.

Hindu thinkers of different schools of philosophy have varying standpoints on what they accept as valid sources of knowledge.

- The Cārvākas admit only one source of valid knowledge: Perception.
- The Bauddhas and Vaiśeṣikas admit two sources: Perception and inference.
- The Sāṅkhyas state three sources: Perception, inference, and verbal testimony.
- The Naiyāyikas also accept a fourth way: Comparison.

- The Prabhākaras add a fifth dimension: Postulation or assumption.
- The Bhaṭṭas and Vedāntins add a sixth source: Non-cognition or non-perception. Non-cognition is the knowledge of the absence of a thing, such as when we say, 'There is no jar in this room.' The Bhaṭṭas and Vedāntins thus accept all six sources of knowledge.

108 PRINCIPAL UPANISHADS

From Ṛg-veda (11)

Aitareya

Akṣa-mālikā

Ātma-bodha

Bahvṛca

Kauśītaki

Mudgala

Nāda-bindu

Nirvāṇa

Sarasvatī-rahasya

Saubhāgya-lakṣmī

Tripura

From *Yajur-veda (Kṛṣṇa Yajur-veda)* (28)

Akṣi

Amṛta-bindu (Brahma-bindu)

Amṛta-nāda

Avadhūta

Brahma

Brahma-vidyā

Dakṣiṇāmūrti

Dhyāna-bindu

Ekākṣara

Garbha

Kālāgni-rudra

Kali-santaraṇa

Kaṭha

Kaṭha-rudra

Nārāyaṇa

Pañca-brahma

Prāṇāgnihotra

Rudra-hṛdaya

Sarva-sāra

Śārīraka

Śuka-rahasya

Skanda

Taittirīya

Tejobindu

Varāha

Yoga-kuṇḍalinī

Yoga-śikhā

Yoga-tattva

From *Yajur-veda (Śukla Yajur-veda)* (21)

Adhyātma

Advaya-tāraka

Bhikṣuka

Bṛhadāraṇyaka

Haṁsa

Īśāvāsya

Jābāla

Kṣurikā

Maṇḍala-brāhmaṇa

Māntrika

Muktika

Nirālamba

Paiṅgala

Paramahaṁsa

Śātyāyana

Subālā

Śvetāśvatara

Tārasāra

Trisikha

Turīyātīta

Yājñavalkya

From *Sāma-veda* (16)

Āruṇeya	*Maitrāyaṇī*
Avyakta	*Maitreya*
Chāndogya	*Rudrākṣa*
Darśana	*Sannyāsa*
Jābāla	*Sāvitrī*
Kena	*Vajrasūcī*
Kuṇḍika	*Vāsudeva*
Mahā	*Yoga-cūḍāmaṇi*

From *Atharva-veda* (32)

Annapūrṇa	*Devī*
Atharva-śikhā	*Gaṇapati*
Atharva-śira	*Gāruḍa*
Ātma	*Gopāla-tāpanī*
Bhasma-jābāla	*Hayagrīva*
Bhāvanā	*Kaivalya**
Bṛhajjābāla	*Kṛṣṇa*
Dattātreya	*Mahānārāyaṇa*
Mahāvākya	*Praṣna*

Māṇḍūkya	*Rāma-rahasya*
Muṇḍaka	*Rāma-tāpanī*
Nārada-parivrājaka	*Śāṇḍilya*
Nṛsiṁha-tāpanī	*Śarabha*
Parabrahma	*Sītā*
Paramahaṁsa-parivrājaka	*Sūrya*
Pāśupata	*Tripura-tāpanī*

* Some sources list *Kaivalya-upaniṣad* under *Kṛṣṇa Yajur-veda*.

NOTE: The information given in the Appendix has been compiled from various sources and has not been verified. Please refer to direct sources for further study.